Bought in
Brookfield, Wisconsin
July 24, 1972
(Lois & Dick's home)
Lindgren

1 of 2

The Feminine Eye

The Feminine Eye

Shana Alexander

The McCall Publishing Company

New York

To

MY EDITORS AT *LIFE*

Philip Kunhardt and Ralph Graves

who closed the Eye and put it out

and George Hunt

who opened it

Contents

Contents

Introduction

❦

THE pieces I wrote in *Life* magazine under the banner "The Feminine Eye" span a definite era, 1964 to 1969, the marrow of the decade. The first one was typed out in a cellar in Atlantic City. My hands shook—twenty years a professional reporter, I was about to make my debut as myself, to say for the first time what I felt personally about events. The typewriter shook, too. Above our heads, in the big Convention Hall, a stomping mob of Democrats was saluting Lyndon Johnson, its invincible new candidate for President. The last-written column, "Flags in the Rain," on page 81, describes a funeral in Washington, D.C. President Nixon led the mourners, and President Eisenhower lay under the flag.

Events of that apocalyptic decade are already light years gone. Bill DuBay—"Evolution of a Rebel Priest," page 11—has evolved into ex-priest, husband, and father. Another clergyman, Dr. King, is dead. So is Senator Kennedy, who may have been evolving faster and farther than anyone of his generation, moving almost with the speed of light. Some of us missed the blaze until the spark had gone out. Myself, I have evolved from writer into editor—subsided might be the better word—and I have moved from *Life* magazine to *McCall's*. To explain why, I have to go back to the beginnings of "The Feminine Eye." We chose that name because it seemed important then for readers to know that the writer whose opinions, crotchets, and glees would hereafter appear on that page was female. Women's Liberation was not invented yet. Such a thing—a woman writing regularly as a woman—had never happened at our magazine. Since my mother had neglected to make the matter of my gender immediately obvious—a writer herself, she knew that in naming children, as in other important choices in life, subtleties of sound and of sentiment come first—the editors of *Life* undertook to rectify Mother's irresponsible vagueness.

For the good fortune of being female, the geneticists tell me I may thank my father. Thank you, Father. Personally, I have always enjoyed being a woman. But as a lifetime journalist, I lived and worked always in a man's world. I liked that, too. Then came the miraculous advent of "The Feminine Eye," and this returned me to the world of women. It taught me to enjoy the companionship of women, and to appreciate them, study them, and try hard to express what women themselves feel, and not what men say they do.

Myself, I have never enjoyed being a woman quite so much as I do right now. Partly, I suppose, that is due to my own age, to the advent of—awful word—maturity. Forty is so much more fun than twenty. (Thirty is unspeakable.) But mostly, I think, it is due to *our* age, to the age we all share, 1970.

I am quite sure that being a woman now, particularly an American woman, is more interesting, challenging, exciting, and rewarding—and more complicated—than it has ever been before. As for being a woman editor, which means talking, and listening, to so vast and varied an audience of other women— well, it's awesome of course, but I like that, too.

That is really why I am at *McCall's* today. Once I was offered the job, I couldn't find good enough reasons to turn it down. I could have said no, but I didn't want to. I wanted to find ways of saying yes. Yes to women. Yes to the idea that women are important. Yes to the idea that women are thinking, feeling beings, different from men, but not less than men, and in many ways today, more interesting than men.

(xii

Introduction

Men are much the same as they were a generation or two ago, but women are changing very fast, in ways we cannot yet quite see. Certainly child-rearing and the housewifely arts do not interest us one bit less, but the world outside the home interests us more. Women know more, they experience more, and they think more than at any time in history.

I studied anthropology in college, and I have always wondered if there are any innate differences between men and women, beyond those you can see in the mirror or, for that matter, on any movie screen. The one difference I feel sure about is that women are by nature conservative, or rather, conservators. Women like to make things, to make environments; they are natural nest-builders. I think this is why women are so deeply involved in the things that can save this country: conservation, education, politics, and the arts. And somehow today I feel that women are more liberated in their minds than men, more idealistic, and often crazily brave.

1

I Like Their Style

The Best First Lady

❦

ROUGHLY speaking, the President of the United States knows what his job is. Constitution and custom spell it out, for him as well as for us. His wife has no such luck. The First Ladyship has no rules; rather, each new woman must make her own. It is as if we hand her hammer and nails, gold leaf, and a bit of bunting and say, "Here. Build the thing yourself."

What was handed to Mrs. Lyndon Johnson was something even less: a wrecked and blasted Camelot haunted by our special vision of its dazzling, martyred queen. Now five difficult years have passed; it is time to go home.

Though Lady Bird is said to be privately delighted by her husband's decision to retire, it is scarcely an upbeat ending for either of the Johnsons. The First Lady has spent the past eight months as a kind of chatelaine, condemned to repair cracked cups, inventory furnishings, and generally tidy things up for the new woman, whoever she might turn out to be. That is an eternity for anyone to have to spend cleaning house, and I was happy when I heard that Mrs. Johnson was going to be able to escape for one last beautification tour.

I caught up with the First Lady and her party on the last gasp of her Last Hurrah—a day of hiking and ceremony among the redwoods of northern California. To see Mrs. Johnson in the depths of that great, primeval, dripping forest is to understand immediately why she is called Lady Bird.

December 1968

Tiny, always a smaller woman than one had quite remembered, she is slimmer now than ever. She twitters. She is cheery, modest, persistent, and alert, and her avian qualities are intensified by those looming, green-black, and ultimately incomprehensible trees. Among them, dedicating the Redwood National Park, Lady Bird in her scarlet coat looked like a jaunty red cardinal.

As usual, some things about her beautification trip were unsettling. One had to fly and drive through miles of man-made pollution to find the natural beauty we had come here to honor, and even as we celebrated its preservation, its destruction continued around us. Smoldering sawdust fouled the skies; paper-mill sludge clotted the bay. On our official bus, official botanists told us that the groves have stood here for two million years. *Sequoia sempervirens*, the tallest and among the oldest living things on earth. The new park, they said, will save them from becoming extinct. But every few moments the bus window wiped black—another timber truck returning from the high hills with two or three giants chained across its back. Their bark stripped, they looked flayed and raw. All day the fat, wet, red logs rolled by.

And this last day was far too full. There was too much here to take in, and too much that was out of human scale, and too many opposites to be reconciled—somewhat like the Great Society itself. Magnificent prehistoric groves pressed against logged-over ridges that looked like a giant's jawbone with the teeth knocked out. There were beach and forest, elk and osprey, Indians and woodcutters, timber barons and conservationists, schoolgirl choirs and grinning politicians, and everywhere, omnipresent, the mystery of the great trees.

Their backs to the sea, these redwoods seemed to be making their last stand. *Sempervirens.* Live forever. This place is really a tree cathedral, sacred to immortality. How strange to wind it all up here, among these prehistoric giants about to fall of their own weight. Though the forest is magnificent, there is something scary in this fern-bottomed, dripping gloom. These trees are really too big. Too old. Some have been dying for two thousand years. A fundamental law of proportion seems broken here, and in one's mind it becomes a magic wood where the most commonplace conversations take on strange overtones. A toppled giant is lying on the forest floor, the underside of its roots obscenely exposed. Nothing is deader than a dead redwood. "No tap root, you see," says a dry voice behind me. "When they tip, they go up like a plate."

"What kind of a wind would it take to turn one over?"

"Depends how exposed they are."

Certainly there is nothing supernatural about Lady Bird. When I caught up with her in another chilly forest amphitheater, it was lunchtime; box lunches on damp benches, and an arc of rough-sawn seats opposing the arc of cameras to watch her chew. She appeared not to notice the photographers, nor the puddle underfoot. What was troubling her was the problem of response. Each time she visits a new place, she said, she catches herself wishing she could scout all her beautification trips beforehand, rather than have the advance work done by members of the White House staff. "Then when they stick that ugly black thing in your face five minutes after you arrive and ask what you think of the redwoods, you would really have something to say."

Who could possibly respond to a redwood, I wondered. And then I thought of all the ugly black things that must have been stuck in her face along the Maine coast, along the Rio Grande and all the other places. How many box lunches had there been? How many historical plaques? How many vistas? How many daffodils? Perhaps if anyone could respond to a redwood, it would be Lady Bird. She may be better equipped than anyone on earth. She has always dwelt among gigantica, in Texas, in the White House, and in history. Few women can ever have been more loomed over.

Somewhere on that last, overcrowded day I saw a five-year diary of Mrs. Johnson's travels: September 1965: planted a tree to dedicate the county courthouse in Peoria; April 1966:

5)

dedicated new esthetic lighting of San Antonio River; September 1966; 100,000 daffodil bulbs, Washington, D.C.; June 1967: National Historic Landmark plaque, home of Calvin Coolidge, Plymouth, Vermont. Individually these achievements seemed modest and rather colorless acts, like Lady Bird herself. But it was a very thick notebook, covering over forty trips, and in the aggregate a heroic achievement. When you add in all the other quiet, half-remembered things Mrs. Johnson had caused to happen, and caused not to happen—her instinctive rush of loyalty to the Walter Jenkins family, for example, or the time she got that dressed-up dog out of the photograph—this quiet, plain, tough little woman looks more and more remarkable. Somewhere in that strange forest on that last day I began to sense how much more Mrs. Johnson leaves behind her than daffodils coast-to-coast. Quite possibly she is the best First Lady we have ever had.

Even Better than Batman

🌾

I HAVE forsaken Batman for a new TV hero who for me has even more POW, more THWUCK than the caped crusader himself. The new man is William F. Buckley, Jr., whose prickly debates heard weekly on his show, *Firing Line*, make far and away the best talk on television.

I like the show for a lot of reasons, beginning with the cheerfully malevolent personality of the star. Buckley is more than the show's hero; he is his own best villain as well. Attacking a choice victim, he is as gleeful as the Joker, and he relies on the same juicy melodramatic tricks—the wildly popping eye, the flicking serpent's tongue, and the richly cultivated voice. His invective is as rich as his voice, and in the field of the screwy epithet Buckley is easily Batman's peer. He once called David Susskind such a staunch liberal that "if there were a contest for the title 'Mr. Eleanor Roosevelt,' he would unquestionably win it."

What really beats Batman is that Buckley is real, and so are his guests—Norman Thomas, Bishop Pike, Barry Goldwater, James Farmer. What beats all the other talk shows is the quality of the talk, which is swift, literate, informed, often witty, and frequently bitchy. I like Buckley because he not only doesn't play fair, he doesn't even pretend to. Good talk, not universal justice, is what Buckley is after, and he knows how to get it.

August 1966

But the clinching reason I like Buckley is that he appears not to give a damn whether I like him or not. In contrast to that cloying, puppy-dog friendliness that characterizes other TV hosts, such aloofness is irresistible.

On a recent trip to New York, I was almost disappointed when the real Mr. Buckley turned out to be a terribly easy man to see. He inhabits an elegant town house just off Park Avenue, and there is something distinctly lairlike about the place. No batpoles, to be sure, but there is a vast, shadowy entrance hall, and a tall, curving banister, with a powerful motorbike parked at its foot. Two parlormaids armed with vacuum cleaners grope around in the gloom, and an unmistakable scent of rose petals hangs in the close air.

Buckley himself is tanned, seersuckered, and charming, and at close range it is evident that his forked tongue is in his cheek a good deal of the time. It is equally apparent that while he is a magazine editor, a syndicated newspaper columnist, a millionaire yachtsman, and an able enough politician to win 340,000 votes in New York's 1965 mayoral election, his true métier is show business.

AFTRA, a show business union, evidently thinks so too and recently demanded he take out a union card. Buckley was outraged. He revenged himself on organized labor by naming as beneficiary of his AFTRA life insurance policy the violently antiunion National Right To Work Committee.

Buckley sees himself as neither a politician nor a performer but as a writer, or more precisely, a rewriter. "I wouldn't show a first draft to anybody, not even my wife," he says. A dedicated quill-pen man at heart, Buckley believes that the mark of a real writer is to become less and less satisfied with the ad-lib form. As a result Buckley is unable to watch, let alone enjoy, his own show. The premiere debate with Norman Thomas delighted me with talk like this: "Mr. Norman Thomas has run six times for President of the United States, and six times the American people in their infinite wisdom have declined to elect him. . . . If I were asked what has been

(8

his specialty in the course of a long career, I guess I would say 'being wrong.' " But the same show threw Buckley into such a blue funk that he has never watched himself again.

The idea for *Firing Line* grew out of four or five taped debates he did in 1964 for Patrick Frawley, the ultraconservative chairman of Eversharp, Inc. But, Buckley commented, "Frawley's idea of a debate is to have Arthur Schlesinger tear open his shirt at the end and cry, 'Mr. Buckley, I repent for all my sins,' " and he has since refined his emceeing techniques.

He now tries to "put a little starch in my introductions," which is how the Mr. Eleanor Roosevelt crack came to be. Buckley says he would have been gentler with Susskind, but he was annoyed at having had so many clichés hurled at him by Susskind when Buckley was a guest on *Open End*. "He always says to me, 'Bill, why don't you move out of the nineteenth century?' That old line has the same depressing effect on me as the first three notes of the Rachmaninoff Prelude. Susskind is a much greater embarrassment to liberals, you know, than he is a goad to conservatives."

Buckley's own greatest satisfaction comes "when I get something said that both needs saying and isn't banal," or "when I can expose an unexpected area of weakness." He liked his interview with presidential speech writer Richard Goodwin because "it showed the schizophrenia between rhetoric and activity at the highest level." He liked debating Staughton Lynd because "when a man tells you the moon is made of green cheese, what is interesting is what makes him think so." He added that he found it interesting that Lynd is the son of two of America's most celebrated sociologists, the authors of *Middletown*.

"Is he their only child?" I asked.

Buckley's Minnie Mouse eyelids flapped. "I hope so," he said.

Although he is aware of TV's inevitable mellowing effect—Buckley himself might prefer the word erosion—on his own viper image, he doesn't know what to do about it. "It's this host business that makes things so difficult," he says. In formal, off-camera debates, he prefers never to meet his opponent beforehand because "it's too emulsifying." Though training and temperament make him expert in the British debating tradition, which he describes as one of "tremendous offstage civility," he claims that something more gladiatorial suits his own bloodthirsty tastes.

I said I admired the delicate way he phrased his cruelest remarks, the feigned tentativeness that masks an absolute certainty.

"You're being oxymoronic," he replied.

There are occasions when it is best to come right out and ask, "What does that word mean?" and this seemed to be one of them.

"Oh, you know," said Buckley. "A black angel. A soft butcher." His eye twinkled. "A liberal Republican."

Evolution of a Rebel Priest

❦

TADPOLE into frog, sketch into statue, tribe into state—evolution is fascinating to watch. To me it is most interesting when one can observe the evolution of a single man. I have had this privilege recently in the case of Father William DuBay, whom I first met in 1964 when he was a callow and unworldly Los Angeles priest.

In less than two years' time the timid priest has evolved into a clerical *cause célèbre*. He has written an important new book, *The Human Church*, which was published without the customary imprimatur and which advocates, among other radical suggestions, a labor union for priests. The book resulted in DuBay being suspended as a priest on orders from his bishop, James Francis Cardinal McIntyre. DuBay responded by sending a direct request to Pope Paul VI that he be given an ecclesiastical trial. If the Vatican denies his request, he says he will take his cardinal into civil court.

The real issue, he claims, is not heresy or even insubordination, but free speech—a topic which seems to be popping up everywhere else these days, but which is still quite a novelty within the Church hierarchy. In the midst of the uproar, DuBay was fired from his job as a hospital chaplain and at once announced that he would move into Synanon House, a beach-front rehabilitation center for dope addicts, where he has been doing counseling work. At his first press conference there

April 1966

DuBay said, "To me, freedom of speech and of belief is more important than freedom to say Mass or administer the sacraments." Then he settled down to await word from Rome.

Evolution may seem a curious term to apply to a priest who gets himself so quickly into such far-out circumstances as these, but I looked the word up, and it means the unfolding or defining of what is already implied. Having watched the way DuBay got started, I find it hard to see how he could have developed along different lines. DuBay is an easy man to describe—he is Wally Cox in a Roman collar—and he got started because of civil rights. I first met him when he wrote an impulsive letter to the Pope urging that Cardinal McIntyre be fired. As a white priest in a Negro parish, DuBay was outraged by the cardinal's failure to take a stand on civil rights.

The outcome of this insurrection was not too surprising. The Vatican managed to ignore his letter, the cardinal said nothing either, and the hotheaded priest eventually was persuaded to renew his vows and then to keep silent. There was something boyish about the whole affair. DuBay admitted he had challenged his cardinal halfway by accident—a group protest of priests was originally planned, but on showdown day, only DuBay turned up—and that he was scared to death. His brave stance reminded me a lot of the shivering kid out on the end of the high diving board who must either jump or crawl back. There are certain kids to whom this classic situation appears really to offer only one choice, not two, and I felt that DuBay was probably one of that kind. I still remember his sincere Wally Cox voice telling me, "I don't want to divide the Church. I don't want to be another Martin Luther."

"Don't worry," I privately replied.

The scandalous new book, the priestly suspension, and the move to Synanon all occurred in rapid succession, and for a couple of days DuBay's face and voice were all over the papers and on TV. These appearances made it quite clear that the tadpole phase had ended. Not only was there a striking new firmness in the voice and manner of the central character in the drama. The issues themselves had resolved into a classic conflict: Should a man bow to authority or obey his conscience? This one turns up all the time on the stage—*Saint Joan, Becket, A Man for All Seasons*—and the playwrights invariably take the same side, possibly because writers by nature inhabit anarchistic and disorderly minds and have no talent for running institutions.

The naïve priest appears to have evolved into a leader, an interesting thinker, and in his tilting with the chancery, a sophisticated gamesman as well. He has also developed a sharp sense of the value of publicity, both to promote his own cause and to protect himself from capricious or harsh buffeting from above. His book seems to me a remarkable ecumenical testament for any clergyman to turn out, but particularly for a once-doctrinaire Catholic priest. He writes, "The Church is not 100 percent human. But it should be. Whatever in it that is not human is not of God." The most startling part of his book is the labor union proposal. But what he is really asking for, I think, is some sort of grievance procedures so that bishops cannot act arbitrarily to prohibit their priests from becoming "involved." And I suspect the use of the word "union," rather than something sedate like "association," was deliberately provocative. When DuBay told a TV interviewer, "I've come to the conclusion that we've got a—ahem—management problem," the closeup camera made the twinkle in his eye unmistakable.

DuBay twinkles almost continually these days, a phenomenon which caused an ex-priest I know to remark, "Most suspended priests are like whipped dogs. That's because the crime is always either Punch or Judy, whiskey or women. But DuBay has no guilt, only a great sense of exuberance." By his own admission, part of this exuberance comes from DuBay's regular participation in Synanon games, an aggressive form of group therapy that is responsible for Synanon's astonishing rate of addict cures. Game players must try to express gut-

13)

level emotions with total honesty. DuBay has been both a leader and a participant in these games for some time, and one way of looking at what has happened to him is to say that his game has escaped from the confines of Synanon and got out into the real world.

This sort of talk would sound a bit far-out even in far more liberal Catholic circles than the Los Angeles diocese. But when DuBay remarks, as he did the other day, that "the ecumenical movement should not be directed toward a consensus of thought, but toward finding ways of accommodating dissent," it seems to me he is directly in line with the dedication of his book, which reads, "In honor of the memory of John XXIII, a Pope who led."

Watching DuBay's evolution, I have often wondered what was really evolving here, a zealot, a reformer, a kook, or just a man. Unquestionably I think the last has occurred, and as a result my own feelings about the propriety of his actions have changed too. Whereas I once thought DuBay was probably obliged to leave the Church if he felt as much defiance as he claimed, I think now that he is probably obliged to remain, which is obviously what he thinks himself.

The Clean Breast and the Fell Swoop

❦

NINETEEN sixty-six was a great year for enigmatic public statements by public figures, and I for one am glad it is over. By year's end, the strain of figuring out what everybody from Dean Rusk to Jacqueline Kennedy to Stokely Carmichael *really meant* had begun to strike me as more trouble than the answer ever was worth. Looking back, 1966 seems to have been the year in which rhetoric swelled as credibility declined, and by mid-December the amount of divination and entrail-gazing demanded by each morning's headlines had reduced me to a state of psychic exhaustion, all intuition spent and my antennae worn down to the very nubs.

It was therefore with great whoops of joy that just before Christmas I read David Merrick's announcement that he was closing his trouble-plagued show *Breakfast at Tiffany's*, twelve days before its Broadway opening and despite an advance sale of nearly one million dollars. I bear no ill will toward anyone connected with this disastrous enterprise, which I gather was one of the least felicitous collaborations in the history of the musical theater. Rather, it was the manner in which Merrick described the disaster that struck me as so utterly praiseworthy. He had decided to close his show, he said, to avoid

January 1967

subjecting "the drama critics and the theatergoing public to an excruciatingly boring evening."

"Since the idea of adapting *Breakfast at Tiffany's* for the musical stage was mine in the first place," he added, "the closing is entirely my fault and should not be attributed to the three top writers [Nunnally Johnson, Abe Burrows, and Edward Albee] who had a go at it. It is my Bay of Pigs."

What a stylish exit! No mingy equivocations, no banal platitudes, not very many words at all. The announcement was splendidly terse, as well as total. A very important part of its charm lay in the use of the personal pronoun: *My* Bay of Pigs, he said, not *our*.

The Merrick statement resurrected what by 1966 had become an almost forgotten mode of public utterance—the one that achieves its character and zest by means of the burnt bridge, the clean breast, the called spade, the fell swoop.

Of course, you have to have a really big and clear-cut disaster on your hands in order to make a bravura gesture of this kind; something on the order of hundreds of thousands of defective automobiles. Or an ever-escalating war that nobody wants. And you also have to have the power to fold your own show, and to sustain the consequences of closing it, which is what puts David Merrick in so much better a position, fell-swoopwise, than Lyndon Johnson.

Another thing you need in order to make a glorious, Merrick-type exit from the field of battle is a genuine free-choice situation. Awful as your show or your product or your service really is, it must be able to endure, at least for a while, in its appalling form. Merrick could have kept going on the strength of his advance sale. In the same manner, the city fathers on smog control boards can keep going because they know that their polluted air, while filthy, is not yet fatal. If they were dealing instead with bubonic plague, they would be forced to act. It is acting for the public good, without being actually forced to, that seems so maddeningly sweet today. Imagine a producer not only knowing that we would be "excruciatingly bored," but admitting it, and even sheltering us from the ordeal!

I have begun to dream up a New Year's list of even more impossibly grand, all-out gestures. The State Department could recognize Red China. Ronald Reagan could put the Berkeley campus under martial law. Selective Service could draft George Hamilton. The collectors of Internal Revenue could tear up Form 1040 and start over. The UFOs could speak up and admit they're out there. William Buckley could quit playing devil's advocate and admit he's a closet liberal. The Pope could give up on birth control. The National Rifle Association could admit that guns kill people, instead of claiming after every tragedy, "No, people kill people." Adam Clayton Powell could come in from the cold. The United Nations could embargo trade with South Africa. New York City could handle its traffic problem by opening fire on all private cars. Bobby Kennedy and J. Edgar Hoover could fight a *mano a mano*. Cassius Clay could walk barefoot to Mecca. The Arabs could acknowledge the presence of Israel. Frustrated city planners and beautification experts could do something really drastic like setting fire to all the billboards and blasting places like Oakland or Newark off the face of the earth.

The sad truth, of course, is that very few people ever have a chance to do what Mr. Merrick had a chance to do, and did so well. Most people lose control of the consequences of their own tastes and acts. This, I think, is what happened to the Kennedys and poor William Manchester. I think the original sin in this case goes back to that treacherous concept, "the authorized version." In retrospect, one can see that an "authorized version" of our national tragedy should never have been commissioned.

Apropos of authorized versions, the definitive 1966 word on that subject was recently issued by the authorized next governor of the state of California. Ronald Reagan's office has distributed a solemn warning to the press to beware of "news releases or other information relating to Governor-elect Reagan issued by unauthorized persons."

"Who are these unauthorized persons?" a newsman who received the memo asked a Reagan aide.

"I'm not authorized to say," Reagan's man replied.

Black Is His Way of Thinking

"O DAY of Palms, Day of Victory, Great GOD, what a Day!" The tall, vigorous pastor exulted, his arms spread wide over his people like some great prehistoric bird, as he strode with majestic, measured tread down the aisle of Harlem's thronged Abyssinian Baptist Church. He wore flowing black robes with crimson Coptic crosses on the breast, and as he paced and wheeled before the vast white marble altar, the powerful yet graceful figure of the Reverend Adam Clayton Powell, Jr., looked naggingly familiar to me. It wasn't that I didn't know who he was. It was who he *looked* like that fussed at my mind.

I had met Powell first on another Sunday twenty-four years ago in the basement of this same building. I was a New York City schoolgirl then, and the children in the Abyssinian Church Sunday school had invited our class to visit them. Earlier in the week, the Harlem youngsters had spent a morning with us. Though I recall their visit vividly, in particular how carefully dressed and how reserved the Negro children were in contrast to our own offhanded ways, I have no corresponding mental picture of our excursion to Harlem, except for one intriguing fact: Their Negro pastor looked completely white. The rest of my childish memory is blank, wiped out perhaps by the historic exclamation point of the date itself, which was 7 December 1941.

April 1965

Powell has continued to impress, amuse, and outrage me on and off ever since. He is still the most popular voice in Harlem, and, according to a poll of the Washington press corps, after twenty-one years as a congressman he remains the least popular voice in Congress. He has been an effective chairman of the House Committee on Education and Labor and, at the same time, a living caricature of the junketing, swinging congressman. But his antics delight his constituents—in their admiring eyes he goes Mr. Charlie one better—and Powell himself says that to live any less exuberantly would be a betrayal of his race. It seems characteristic of his own gaudy style of doing things that he could write a thoughtful magazine piece advocating a code of ethical practices for congressmen, then deposit the check in his wife's account to avoid payment of a libel judgment against him.

When he jubilantly announced that, after five months of exile from New York to avoid the $52,000 libel judgment, he would return to Harlem to preach once more, I knew I wanted to be there too. Powell has always had a fine flair for theatrics, and I thought it was not entirely a coincidence that his triumphal and virtuous reentry into the city had been set for Palm Sunday.

By the time I got to the handsome old Gothic church, over three thousand people were crowded inside—platoons of dignified deacons, matrons in flowery hats, local pols, babies to be blessed, even Powell's bail bondsman was there—and I don't think he let a single one of us down.

Two services were needed to handle the crowds. The Reverend Wyatt T. Walker, Powell's new assistant, who until recently was Martin Luther King's assistant, preached first, while Powell sat at the rear of the pulpit chuckling with admiration. When Walker finished, Powell began joyfully stalking the aisles, arms spread wide, calling for new members to join his church. "This is the happiest day of my life," he cried.

A woman came down the aisle and he called, "Come on,

(20

sweetheart, take my hand!" He shouted up to the choir loft, "Sing it, Charlie," then, back at the beaming congregation, "Take my hand. The pastor's back. Pastor's back in town!" For all their religious fervor, those moments were a lot like Carol Channing's second-act entrance in *Hello, Dolly!*

Powell began his own service with a solemn prayer. He looked like an ancient, awesome Coptic priest as he intoned, "Lo, the dreamer cometh. He was unworthy. Through thirty-five years of preaching in this place he has become worthy." Then he rolled out his title—"Think Big, Think Black, Think Like a Child of God"—and began to preach. Under "Think Big," he told us that as a little Harlem kid he dreamed, "One day I'll be in Congress. Today I control the labor legislation in this country. I control the war on poverty. The President asked for two billion. I'm gonna push for three. Think big."

Under "Think Black," he said, "Nobody is better than you are. No matter what Mr. Charlie said, you're Mr. Black. Black is a way of thinking." He grinned and pointed at the light-skinned Reverend Wyatt Walker. "Yellow Negroes like you and myself, we *gotta* think black." The congregation roared with delight.

The passage on "Think Like a Child of God" brought Powell the Baptist preacher onstage: "The Negro is no better than white folks, but he knows God better. . . . What a day! What a day of victory. Every day from now on gonna be Palm Sunday. All the stars are singing together. All the trees are clappin' their hands. Oh, what the future holds for me!"

Powell neatly mixed secular and clerical in a closing pitch for funds. "I'm here only temporarily. Unless the judgment is paid, I cannot stay here." He told us that friends and parishioners had already raised $16,000, and added, "I believe that with your prayers and cooperation everything will be wiped out this month." By that time I had absolutely no doubt of it.

At a press conference following his sermon, Powell was a politician straight out of *The Last Hurrah*. When he was asked

21)

about speculation that he might run for mayor of New York, he said, "I am a humble parish priest." Asked his opinion of Martin Luther King, he said, "Martin Luther King is the greatest living human being, black or white, in the world today, but we don't need him in Harlem."

Later I had a brief private audience with the pastor in his robing room. He was wearing a T-shirt now, his clerical dickey was askew, and he looked relaxed, happy, and very fit. I congratulated him on his sermon, and he said, "Ah, yes, it has all come to pass. I am the old man of the black revolution." He lit a cigarette, and as I watched the smoke curl up past his rakish black mustache, I finally knew whom it was he reminded me of: the *Show Boat* gambler, Gaylord Ravenal, right after a really successful boat ride.

Yet for all the flimflam, Powell has been a vigorous and responsible civil-rights crusader for thirty-five years. He has preached and practiced nonviolent direct social action since the 1930s, and he is still the most interesting and politically effective Negro leader today. I do not find him the most admirable, and one might wish he had served Harlem better. But few others have served Harlem at all.

2

I Like These Things

Dublin Is My Sure Thing

❦

WHAT does a lady who travels a lot require of her favorite city?

It should be remote but accessible, unhackneyed but urbane. It should please the eye in its vistas and proportions, yet be modest enough in scale not to overwhelm the traveler who likes to stroll about on foot. Its populace must speak a language in which the strolling lady also can converse, and they should be a people of special charm, wit, courtesy, and learning. The weather there should refresh, dress should not be demanding, and diversions should be limited but piquant. The city should have a rich tradition of history and literature. The citizenry should include uncommon numbers of poets.

There is such a city. It is Dublin. The mark of a true crush, whether the object be man, woman, or city, is that you fall in love first and grope for reasons afterward, and that is what happened a few years ago with me and Dublin. I still don't know Dublin well; we have only met three brief times; I am still groping. I like the graceful Georgian streets and squares, a series of steel engravings under wet skies. "Long, haggard corridors of rottenness and ruin," O'Casey called these same streets, which house some of the meanest slums in the world, but I am a tourist and see only fanlights and facades. I like the

September 1966

green and lavender light, the many pubs, the sound of the voices, the gallows humor, and the queer intimacy with disaster that makes this city the place where putting one's head in the lion's mouth is the archetypal municipal gesture, and where the one-wheel skid on the brink of catastrophe is the accepted way of life.

A small but perfect example of this occurred a moment after our plane touched down at Dublin Airport. We were making our way in single file across the wet, blowy field when an Aer Lingus clerk dashed out of the terminal and asked the first person in line where our plane had just come from. "Paris," said the passenger, and the clerk thanked him and rushed back to post the correct notice and flight number beside our arrival gate.

I was at once glad to be back. Everything looked sparkling to me, though a friend apologized "for the terrible pall of gloom that hangs over the town." He explained with regret that a marathon eighty-four-day bank strike had just been settled. Despite the inconvenience, Dubliners had viewed the strike as a great mercy because the banks couldn't lose, the public couldn't lose, and while it lasted, everybody lived on credit. When people ran out of money they wrote checks. Cash piled up in great heaps, and talk was that crime had dropped away to nothing because with unlimited credit there was no longer any need to steal. A great glow of good feeling had embraced the city. One drinker gazed fondly down at the blank check he had just obtained from the publican and asked, "How many 0s in ten thousand?"

The major theatrical event in Dublin during my visit was a revival of O'Casey's classic Dublin tragedy, *Juno and the Paycock*, put on by Peter O'Toole. The production had a gorgeous potential for disaster on many levels. Today the play creaks a bit at the joints, but it is also the Old Master's old masterpiece, and to attempt it in Dublin is like putting on Chekhov in Moscow. O'Toole is physically wrong for the part, and he lacks the Dublin accent. Sick actors, botched

(26

rehearsals, and vanishing scenery complicated things still more. But somehow, barely, it all came together. O'Toole and his brilliant costars, Siobhan McKenna and Jack McGowran, flung themselves into their parts with such fierce intensity that another player remarked, "Irish actors don't really want to act. They want to win." He was right, and they did win. The packed Gaiety Theatre rang with applause—"We clapped them in and we'll clap them out!" my neighbor shouted—and the evening ended with strings of curtain calls and massive festivities around the city that lasted until dawn.

It was a glorious night and it was O'Toole himself who gave the best description of the city's strange appeal. "A dangerous village," he said, waving his skinny arm toward Dublin's moon-lit rooftops. "Weird. It's not Ireland. There's no thought here. If you think, you go potty. You must get your work done, pull your hat over your eyes, put up the collar, and get out. The trap is the Irishness. It's a hump on your back, but sweet too. It's all so gorgeous. The afternoon here is Russian, like walking in cotton wool. And oh, the chat!"

The chat remained gorgeous to the very end. A friend took me to see The Brazen Head, Dublin's oldest tavern, and we paused in the dark, low-ceilinged bar to read a framed copy of the last words of Robert Emmet. "I am going to my cold and silent grave; my lamp of life is nearly extinguished. . . . My race is run," my companion beautifully read aloud.

"The grave opens to receive me, and I sink into its bosom," said a solitary workingman drinking Guinness at the end of the bar. He was speaking from memory, not reading from the wall. "But they've glamorized it a bit, haven't they?" he continued. "The English court reporter fixed it up. Not even Robert Emmet could speak like that." There ensued an informed and lively debate over the niceties of the eighteenth-century rhetorical tradition and the precise details of Emmet's guerrilla tactics, and a discussion of the kinds of social forces that breed patriots and traitors—barroom chat I cannot imagine in any other city.

Nor can I imagine elsewhere the Sunday family scene in another pub when a waiter accidentally dumped a glass of Pernod over the head of an elderly poet seated at a low table with his wife and daughter. The fiery baptism flowed in all directions, and the poet bent double, dabbing at his eyes and blowing like a walrus.

"Oh, Dominic," exclaimed the wife, at once putting things right again. "Such a fine, great head you have. The drink sprayed right off it and not a drop touched your Sunday suit."

On another morning I watched a man begin his day with a glass of Irish coffee. His hand trembled rather violently as he lifted the cream-topped brew to his lips, and glancing down at it, he observed with interest, "Whitecaps!"

I left the dangerous village later that same morning, happy as larry and still groping for reasons why. As I was walking once more across the blowy airfield, it occurred to me that at the end of my third visit to my favorite city, my score was three out of three. Dublin is my sure thing. It always works. It's the spa that always cures, the slot machine that always pays off. I don't say it will work for you. Go find your own city. Dublin is mine.

A Delicious Appeal to Unreason

SOME people swear by hot water and lemon; others favor setting-up exercises. For me, a swift glance at my horoscope in the morning newspaper is the preferred way to start the day. Faithful horoscope-watching, practiced daily, provides just the sort of small but warm and infinitely reassuring fillip that gets matters off to a spirited start.

My devotion to syndicated advice is not slavish; if the forecaster ever came out and said bluntly, "Today is a mess. Stay in bed," I would probably ignore him and chance getting up anyhow. But the lovely thing is that he never does say that. There is no such thing as a bad horoscope. There are dull ones and murky ones, to be sure. "Don't procrastinate. Get right at it," was this morning's cheerless word. But predictions of out-and-out disaster are unknown to readers of syndicated astrology columns. And there are many mornings when just this guaranteed absence of doom, printed right there in newspaper black-and-white, is a great deal more heartening than, say, a hot cup of coffee.

I am not an occult nut. Ouija boards, poltergeists, and spirit rappings leave me unmoved. Plain newspaper horoscopes, plus an occasional fortune cookie, have always satisfied my appetite for knowing what was going to happen next. Then two years ago, almost inadvertently, I embarked on a fortune-telling

May 1966

binge. A friend introduced me to the famous British clairvoyant Maurice Woodruff, who offered to give me a reading. As he laid out the cards, he even suggested I take notes. Later I stuck the piece of paper in the back of a drawer and forgot about it.

By the time I found the notes a couple of months later, it had all begun to happen: I had already lost the earring, and got the traffic ticket, and the man whose initials were G or H had radically changed my life. I wished desperately that I'd taken detailed notes instead of sketchy ones. In nearly two years' time, three-fourths of the items on the piece of paper had actually happened, so when I was in London a few weeks ago, I telephoned Woodruff to arrange for a refill on my prophecy.

England, as well as America, is experiencing a fortune-telling boom, and I had to wait three days for an appointment. Of course I waited. To consult one of Britain's two thousand other full-time practicing fortune-tellers would have been unthinkable. I *like* Woodruff; we are *simpatico*. With clairvoyants, as with dressmakers and with psychiatrists, that *simpatico* feeling makes all the difference.

Settled finally in the snug office of "my" clairvoyant, an electric heater glowing in one corner, a huge black cat dozing beside it, my notebook expectantly open on the battered desk beside his worn deck of cards, I felt for a moment extremely silly. Then he told me to cut the cards. "An extremely good cut, but a very busy cut . . ." he said in the well-remembered, high, cheery voice, and in a few moments I was scribbling furiously, thoroughly hooked.

"You already have two jobs. By 2 July you'll be offered a third job—nothing to do with writing. I see a person with the initials G or J and H"—so he was back—"who will ask you to represent a firm or a product or a person. You'll want to say, 'But how can I possibly take on that job, too?' But remember, there's no sentiment in business. . . . Your mother wears spectacles, doesn't she? Well, they want changing. . . . I see your husband as two people rolled into one. . . . You will

(30

cross five waters this year, and I guarantee you'll be back here before October. . . . You will visit a Latin country. . . . Your health is on the whole excellent, but in three weeks you will have a little dose of flu. . . ." On and on it went. I have fourteen pages of notes. The last of them says, triumphantly, "You left your last really bad year behind you in 1961 or '62." I walked out of the office certain he was right, and feeling great.

I was far across water from London, indeed I was floating down the Rio Grande one sunny afternoon some days later with Lady Bird Johnson and a party of reporters, when I fell out of our rubber raft. This was nothing surprising—everyone had been tumbling in and out of the rafts all afternoon—but as I clambered to my feet on the right-hand bank of the river, a park ranger called out, "How do you like Mexico, ma'am?"

"The Latin country!" I thought at once. "It's begun!" A few hours later, chilled and weary from the ducking, I was not in the least surprised to feel flu set in. The germs didn't arrive in exactly three weeks, but they stayed with me for exactly three weeks, and when you're dealing with prophecy, you don't quibble over prepositions. While I was convalescing and fretting over the dust gathering on my typewriter, a volunteer nurse asked what subject I would be writing about if I felt well enough to write. "Horoscopes," I rasped weakly.

"Quick, give me the day and date and hour of your birth," she demanded. "I want to send it to my mother in Salt Lake City. She is a great student of astrology." In due course, five typed pages of astrological predictions arrived from Salt Lake. That they were every bit as accurate as the London forecast had been, and that there were no internal contradictions between the two reports, did not surprise me, my nurse, or her mother in the least.

Once you become comfortable thinking astrologically, opposites are reconciled, paradoxes are explained, and everything neatly fits. That is what makes astrology such a satisfactory sort of business. There are days when anyone who detects any pattern in the universe seems worth giving attention to. Only no pattern is truly intolerable. On those days, astrology becomes a delicious appeal to unreason and all the more delectable because within itself it makes sense. At such times, the kind or caliber of sense doesn't matter. The web it weaves must just hang together well enough to snare people like my nurse and her mother and Woodruff and me and my mother. (My mother's glasses did need fixing, of course.)

I have been sitting at this dusty, rusty typewriter all day trying to get at just what it is that people like us understand, as opposed to people like my husband, who vehemently denies that he is two people rolled into one, although I have been telling him exactly the same thing for years. What we basically understand, and accept, I think, is that there is not only no such thing as a bad horoscope, there is no such thing as a wrong one. There are only degrees of rightness. And if I had not spent today "procrastinating," in spite of the warning in my morning newspaper, I feel quite sure now that I could have "got at" this pleasantly simpleminded idea with a good deal more grace and speed.

Neglected Kids—the Bright Ones

❧

THERE is a unique school in my neighborhood to which only nice, normal, healthy little geniuses need apply. This school, a nonprofit institution, happens to be interested exclusively in the education of what are called "gifted" children. A poor word, perhaps, but less offensive to me than, say, "exceptional children," a common euphemism for "retarded." (An equally hideous term is "senior citizens.") At any rate, this particular school accepts only students of stratospheric mental ability uncomplicated by any emotional or physical handicaps. The narrow and glorious aim of the establishment is to make smart kids smarter.

Surprisingly, this simple objective seems to frighten and offend many people, including parents and children at the school. Special, mind-stretching curricula and individualized instruction are expensive—$1,250 a year. At the last PTA meeting, a fund-raising theater party for additional scholarships was being discussed when one mother wailed, "But if I help sell tickets, I'll have to tell all my friends what this school is really for!"

The sad truth is that excellence makes people nervous. What was also troubling this mother, I suppose, was the notion that special education for the specially gifted is somehow "un-

June 1966

democratic." It appears to be setting up an intellectual elite. It smacks somehow of the dirty word "discrimination."

Specialists in the education of gifted children have become accustomed to all sorts of Alice-in-Wonderland opposition. Many public-school officials, for example, feel that isolating the very high IQ youngsters unfairly deprives the average ones of their stimulating company. They also feel that it is detrimental to very bright children to "set them apart socially." Money earmarked for the education of gifted children is almost impossible to come by. Public funds gravitate not to the specially gifted but to the specially handicapped. The State of California, for example, allots forty extra educational dollars per year for each gifted child, and about one thousand dollars per year for each retarded child. Of the several thousand private schools in the United States, specializing in everything from skiing to schizophrenia, less than half a dozen of them are dedicated exclusively to gifted children.

The usual American attitude toward gifted children is reflected in this excerpt from the newest catalog issued by our top publisher of educational handbooks and private-school directories. Under the heading "Mental and Emotional Deviates," one reads the following list of subheads: "the intellectually gifted, brain injured, cerebral palsied, hemiplegic, epileptic, emotionally disturbed and juvenile delinquent, mentally handicapped, aged, narcotic and alcoholic."

I suppose intellectually gifted children are in a sense "mental deviates." But they are also our most important national resource, more important even than our fields and rivers, our vanishing wilderness and disappearing wildlife. Most important, they are our own best legacy to future generations.

The argument that exceptionally gifted children do need a specialized kind of education seems quite persuasive to me. It is not a matter of setting up an elite, but of recognizing that vast, innate differences in children exist, and of devising special school programs that will take these differences into account. Keen competition brings forth one's best efforts, on the tennis court or in the classroom. When very bright children are kept with average youngsters, they are cheated of the mental stimulation they need to develop their full capacities. The experts I have talked to say that putting bright children into the company of their peers does not create intellectual snobs. Rather, it tends to have a humbling effect by showing the whiz kids their own limitations for the first time. As to the bugaboo about "setting children apart socially," it seems worth recalling that the primary purpose of school is learning. Socializing can take place at home, on the block, in the neighborhood.

I know nothing more thrilling than to visit a jumping classroom in full swing. When students are really learning, the teacher carefully framing his questions so as to stay just far enough ahead of his pupils to lead them on, a mutual exhilaration is generated so strong that anyone can detect it. It ionizes the atmosphere. You sense it regardless of subject matter or of the students' capacities. I have felt it while auditing a medical school seminar of which the subject matter was to me totally incomprehensible, and again in a special class of severely handicapped autistic children who were just, finally, discovering the meaning of the word "hug." The same exhilaration was in the air when I dropped into a class of five-year-olds at the gifted children's school.

A session in phonics was under way and the teacher asked, "Can any of you think of a word in which the letter *c* is pronounced not like *k* but like *s?*"

At once ten little hands shot into the air. "Certainly!" said the first child. "Cinnamon!" said the next.

The row of upraised, eager little arms waved like undersea fronds. Learning was a game so exciting to these children that in an instant they were all giggling and wiggling and even trying to attract the teacher's attention by tickling her under the chin as she strolled between the tiny desks.

"Is it all right if the *c* is inside the word?" one little girl wanted to know.

The teacher nodded. "Exceptional!" she piped while I was

35)

still puzzling. But the kid who really won me, and who illustrated the kinship of the normal to the gifted child, was the boy whose hand shot up next.

"I have a word where there's a *c* that sounds like an *s* and a *c* that sounds like a *k* in the same word."

Don't you know what it is? Neither did I, until the freckled little face split wide in a grin and he said, joyfully, "Circus!"

Wishbones and Falling Stars

❦

As a child I loved wishbones and falling stars, Gypsies and ghosts, and I would still rather buy a $100 horoscope than a $100 hat. Once I made a major commitment with the help of a plate of fortune cookies, and when I first visited Greece, I headed straight for the Delphic oracle. (As I knelt over the purifying pool, my sunglasses fell in, an omen which continues to mystify me, though it may come clear to some future traveler.) All that was long ago, but I still feel on warm terms with the supernatural, and when I heard that a big national symposium entitled "Extrasensory Perception—Fact or Fantasy?" was to be held right in my own neighborhood, I made sure to attend.

ESP has finally become respectable, or at least enough so that UCLA was willing to sponsor the two-day meeting as part of its adult education program and to provide its largest campus meeting hall to handle the crowd. Nearly nine hundred of us turned up, at twenty-five dollars a head, and looking around the auditorium, I decided we were what the psychologists call a well-randomized group. One or two were people like the lady who whispered to me that she was kept under constant surveillance by six invisible agents from U.S. Steel. But the majority looked like either graduate students or solid citizens, and a few were professional aerospace men and Air Force scientists in mufti. One of these, from Houston, assured me that many more of his hometown colleagues would have turned out had not UCLA chosen the same weekend that the Gemini astronauts were in orbit.

Looking back, I think the ESP symposium was a great place for me to spend that long and tense weekend. While Majors White and McDivitt adventured in outer space, those of us in the auditorium explored inner space, an area just as vast and uncharted and, to me at least, equally thrilling. Our guides were a distinguished panel of philosophers, psychiatrists, psychologists, neurologists. Not all were persuaded that ESP exists, nor am I myself. What was more impressive than any hard evidence of ESP turned up by the symposium was the fact that serious scientists were willing to debate the topic. As one of them put it, "Scientists with half-closed minds are not scientists at all."

We began by learning the vocabulary. ESP may manifest itself as telepathy (direct mind-to-mind communication); clairvoyance (object-to-mind or event-to-mind communication); precognition (foreseeing the future), or psychokinesis (the power of mind over matter, such as causing dice to fall a certain way). None of these things is the same as intuition, which was defined as the subliminal sensory—not extrasensory —cues that bubble up from the unconscious mind, or "what your wife has."

I don't know about your wife, but I couldn't get through the day without intuition. I trust mine because I have to— there is no time to figure out every decision logically—and because experience suggests it more or less works. Will my fan belt hold out until the next freeway exit? Dare I stay in the shower and just let the phone ring? How should I know? But flying blind this way is exhausting work, and I feel it entitles me to the psychic nourishment of an occasional fortune cookie.

The panel's evidence that some sort of genuine ESP does exist was impressive. We heard a glowing, firsthand report on the Soviet experiments in dermo-optical perception—reading and distinguishing colors through the skin—and there was an even more fantastic account of a test subject in Prague who, under hypnosis, is able to guess the color of cards inside sealed envelopes with an accuracy that exceeds mathematical probability by one in ten-to-the-thirty-fifth power. We learned that hypnosis, like a shot of LSD or a touch of schizophrenia, seems to improve ESP performance. ESP was likened to drawing ability, in that everybody has it, but some people have it far more strongly than others. It works best when the subject is relaxed, confident, and highly motivated to succeed. Years of careful laboratory testing of ESP ability have shown that if you feel lucky, you will be luckier; that if you want strongly to win, your chances of winning improve, and that if you are emotionally hung up some other way, you are also apt to be hung up ESP-wise. To a measurable extent wishing does make it so, something which Las Vegas, if not UCLA, has suspected for some time.

Sex differences were not on the agenda, but I took a private poll of the panel and found that all the experts felt certain that women have greater ESP than men. Two male psychoanalysts theorized that ESP was a feminine trait because it depended on receptivity and openness. But as it happened, most of the symposium's pro-ESP laboratory evidence was presented by a couple of female psychologists, one of whom has spent twenty years testing psychic ability. When I asked these ladies their own opinions, each confessed she had never detected one jot of ESP in herself.

By the time the symposium ended, we had heard many disturbing facts, but no one could offer a unifying theory to explain them. "A fact is not a fact to a scientist *unless* he can explain it," a woman near me remarked, and I said I was very glad just then not to be a scientist. They have to be skeptical; I don't. It seems to me that a person in my position, one who doesn't know too much, is always better off being a believer. Rather than believe nothing, I would rather believe everything until shown otherwise. I think you get just as close to truth my way, and certainly learn more, and probably have a lot more excitement and fun.

The symposium closed with an audience poll. How many had come here already tending to believe in ESP? How many had been skeptical? The question carried a high emotional charge. Proof of ESP in all its forms would force science to alter its concepts of time and space and even death. The show of hands indicated we were about equally divided. Now, had the evidence presented over the past two days caused any people to change their minds? A scant half-dozen hands were raised.

As I was leaving the hall, I met the bearded sage and mystic Gerald Heard. To face the implications of the unknown without flinching, he told me, was "to feel oneself but a wingless gnat in the cupped palm of Pan." His image made me shiver, I didn't know why.

Monday night, as I watched the Gemini landing on TV, I reflected again on the strange bond between the weekend's events on the ground and events overhead. Then I saw that stumpy, tiny capsule bobbing helplessly on the waves, and I knew instantly what it reminded me of. Again I shivered. It looked exactly like a wingless gnat, and I felt overwhelmingly glad the poor-looking thing had made a safe landing.

The Ping's the Thing

🌺

THE first thing I hear each morning, after the alarm clock, is a rich auditory stew of bathroom sounds and radio news, a contrapuntal play-off of running water against solemnly intoned accounts of world catastrophe. Most mornings, the bulletins click past routinely, the regular daily metronome of war, scandal, and freeway crashes—and once in a great while, the authentic gong of tragedy does break through. As rare as the gong is the sort of news item, often trivial, that emits a special, not quite subliminal ping. This ping seems to signal that something funny, or weird, or maybe even profound may have just occurred; one is never quite sure.

A ping went off the other morning when I heard about the Satanic wedding just staged by some people in San Francisco. There had been a bride dressed in scarlet, the altar was the body of a nude woman, hymns to Pan were chanted, in short—the whole diabolical works.

Supplemental details were in the morning paper. The high priest, I read, had been Anton LaVey, for the past fifteen years the Bay Area's only admitted practicing sorcerer, and recently the founder there of a Satanic cult. His marriage service had featured bell, book, and candle, stuck in a human skull; a green-eyed witch with a bronze chalice, and many other ancient and

February 1967

authentic magical props alongside the nude altar. That one, he explained, symbolized devotion to indulgence rather than abstinence.

The altar herself, a twenty-one-year-old redhead who had reclined on a leopard skin atop a stone mantelpiece, had commented after the ceremony, "It was awfully hot up there," and asked for a glass of water.

I never quite got used to this jarring clash between exotic and banal, not even when I got to know the high priest personally. This sorcerer is in the phone book. Such a pity I couldn't attend Anton's regular Friday night Magic Circle meeting, Mrs. LaVey said when I called. (*Mrs.* LaVey? Yes, the sorcerer is married. His household includes two daughters and a five-hundred-pound lion.) But Mrs. LaVey suggested that I visit the family on Sunday and come for a drive in the country. The Satanic wedding had been such a success, she explained, that they were eager to try their hand at staging a black-magic ritual out of doors. They had been thinking of a witches' Sabbath, on *Walpurgisnacht*, but needed a suitably isolated and rustic location.

"Are you, er, a witch, too?" I inquired.

"Well, let's just say a sorceress," Mrs. LaVey replied. "*Witch* has sort of the connotation of cooky-lady now."

Anton LaVey is a tall man with a shaven skull, Mephistophelian beard, and a rich personality. He met me at the airport wearing a leopard-fur vest, a luminous tie, and a ring set with a golf-ball-sized stone faceted in trapezoids. LaVey's studies have revealed that the trapezoid is the most evil shape there is, he told me as we motored back to his house. It is the traditional window into the fourth dimension, the shape of altar stones used in human sacrifice, of the mansard roofs of haunted houses, of the cloven hoof, of magical touchstones, of the cross-section of coffins, and of the Golden Gate Bridge. The very word *hex* means six, and a hexagon is composed of two trapezoids. *Hex* is also the German word for witch. Angles are traditionally symbolic of evil, while curves are symbolic of good. "Think about Christ and the devil," he said. "The nimbus of one is the halo; the other wears horns."

By the time I had thought about all this, we had arrived at the house and been greeted by Mrs. LaVey, a charming and beautiful sorceress with waist-length blond hair and a vinyl plastic miniskirt. We sat in the front parlor (the scene of the wedding), which contains a cloven hoof, sliding panels, creaking doors, a stuffed ocelot and a shrew, pentagrams, freak pictures, goats, gongs, a skeleton—the whole marvelous clutter of magical paraphernalia. Anton and I chatted while Mrs. LaVey went out to the corner grocery to buy breakfast. "After all, what is evil?" he asked. "One church's devils have usually been another church's gods."

The distinguishing feature of his new Satanic religion is that it has no concept of sin, hence it evokes no guilt. "My church teaches love-and-hate. We must learn to hate properly, and with a whole heart."

"Anton says we must accept each slavering monster from the pit and greet him as our friend," Mrs. LaVey remarked, bringing in a tray of ham-and-cheese sandwiches.

Founding a new religion, LaVey has begun to discover, takes more than theory. Fortunately he has skilled professional help. His disciples include a former Billy Graham organizer, an IBM engineer, several university professors of anthropology, and members of the police force, the state government, medicine, the ministry, and the bar. He recently ordained fifteen priests and priestesses of his own, and the group is now preparing a Black Mass LP record, as well as a Satanist Bible.

LaVey takes black magic seriously and sees himself as a true magus in the tradition of Mesmer, Cagliostro, and Rasputin. He has scant use for those witches who practice what he scornfully refers to as white magic. "That old Sybil Leek," he says of the most famous English witch, "why, she has all the power of a busted, secondhand Hoover vacuum cleaner."

Now it was time to leave and start hunting for the right patch of woods. While the sorcerer excused himself to Norelco his head, Mrs. LaVey took me on a tour of their revolving fireplace, black boudoir, and booby-trapped closet, then popped a TV dinner into the oven for her teen-age daughter. After flinging a couple of cut-up raw roosters to the lion roaring in the back yard, we set off.

As we drove along, Anton said he started out in life as an assistant lion tamer for Clyde Beatty, and doubled as the circus calliope player. "Between the music and the wild beasts, it was rather an Orpheus-like existence," he mused.

I asked exactly how he intended to observe *Walpurgisnacht*. "Actually, ritual is the least of my worries," LaVey said. "My big problem right now is to get this new religion off the ground. For *Walpurgisnacht* I'll probably invoke Satan in a solemn ritual, use the flail, scourge the flesh, and drink from the chalice. Then I'll strike the bell eleven times to purify the air and spin counterclockwise to purify the house. After that I'll hold up my sword to the West and invoke Satan, bring in the black goat, chant the names of the four princes of hell in the secret magical language, etcetera, etcetera."

Twilight had begun, and LaVey looked anxiously out of the station-wagon window at the darkening landscape. "What we really need to find now," he said, "is a sylvan glade, a pool, an area for capering, and some good trees to hide behind. Then we'll be free to engage in the revelry."

"Freer than Halloween?" I asked.

"Oh, much freer," he replied. "Halloween is common knowledge. The great thing about *Walpurgisnacht* is that nobody *knows* it's a holiday."

LaVey peered out of the window again. "Nothing is more fun than clandestine activity," he said.

Faintly over the violet hills I heard it. A distant but unmistakable p-i-i-n-g.

More Monsters, Please!

🌷

Shy, hairy, and seven-and-one-half-feet high, the gentle creature ambled out of its California forest, turned to glance at the running cameraman, and sloped off into the primeval gloom, munching berries. It was not a giant ape. It went erect like a human, looked back with a graceful turn of waist and, bending, revealed breasts. When she had gone, a vile odor hung in the mountain air.

Still running, the cameraman arrived in New York with what he said was the first color movie of a Sasquatch, one of a legendary race of enormous humanoids that have been "sighted" more than a hundred times from California to Alaska. Not surprisingly, the film of the monster is blurred, and many scientists who have viewed it are skeptical. Still, the story made newspaper headlines, and surely readers other than myself lingered lovingly over each outlandish detail—the huge "humanoid" footprints fourteen-and-a half inches long, the breasts, the quizzical expression, the bounding gait, the overpowering stink.

Not much of a monster, perhaps, by the old classical standards. But times are lean. The mythological beast, a breed as ancient as man himself, is nearly extinct. Today's garden of possible monsters is a sadly empty zoo, containing only a few Himalayan yetis, some Scottish sea serpents, California's fur-

December 1967

coated humanoids, and an occasional undependable blob up from the ocean floor.

Science has sabotaged fable: Minotaur, dragon, basilisk, phoenix, chimera, mermaid, and sphinx all now are gone. How one longs for them still to be real, still to plunge or plod through trackless wastes, to writhe and rattle the darkening air, to blaze, roar, and mystify, or just to vanish with a wink of tail.

Unicorns perhaps lasted longest. They remained real for four thousand years. Herodotus saw them, and Pliny describes how they foiled hunters with a miraculous somersaulting trick—pitching headlong off the highest cliffs, they could land head down and unharmed, an arrow in earth, upon the twanging horn. Queen Elizabeth I, always a greedy woman, paid an explorer a hundred thousand pounds for a unicorn horn. Rereading about it in Marianne Moore, I still think it money well squandered. With its moonbeam throat and miraculous elusiveness, the unicorn has come to be unique:

> "impossible to take alive,"
> tamed only by a lady . . . like itself—
> as curiously wild and gentle.

Marianne Moore is our century's greatest anatomist of creatures, mythological and real, and my own favorite poet. In her celebrated definition of poetry, Miss Moore said it was the art of making imaginary gardens with real toads in them. What sort of garden, I wonder, would she make for great, shaggy, ridiculous Sasquatch?

The key word about Sasquatch may be "humanoid," a term lovely because it contains "man" in it. The Abominable Snowman endears for the same reason. These "humanoids" make the most satisfying modern monsters because they retain at least the possibility of existence. They might be real. *Something* has been seen, and impaired as the sighting invariably is, "possible" monsters have an enchanting plausibility. One is far less drawn

(46

to metal robots, eight-eyed weirdos from outer space, things doodled by electrical engineers. Entirely unreal monsters, I think, appeal only to children or to the tots in ourselves. They are flat and shallow as horror comics, and just as quickly uninteresting.

The one exception I know to this rule is the seven-ton, saucer-shaped, ivory-colored blob, twenty feet long and matted with woolly hair, which turned up a few years ago on an Australian beach. Although the thing was partially decomposed, naturalists who examined it reported a "gullet" and some slits resembling fish gills, "though it lacked both bone structure and eyes." The absolutely terrifying aspect of this monster was that it was so completely unlike anything.

Man has always needed monsters, and he still does. Our mythical beasts are part of the need to know what we are, to find the monstrosity from which we arose—the missing link, the hairy thighs. But coeval with our need of him is the monster's own need to escape. That is why there is always some impairment in the one who sights the monster. He is drunk, he is running for his life, he is five years old, his camera is defective, he is blinded by the snow or mad from three days in the desert. All this is as it should be. A monster should be heard but not seen. Not quite. The fog, flames, or chasm between it and us are more than traditional. They are mandatory. A monster must be dimly glimpsed. In this connection, I cite two quasi-mythological encounters of my own. Each occurred in blinding sunshine, while I was bottom-fishing from a cockleshell dinghy off the beach at Santa Monica. Once I struggled for three hours to bring up from the depths on inadequate tackle some unknowable weight which, inched at last to the surface and barely glimpsed only in the last split instant before my line broke, turned out to be, I think, a doormat. The other time, only a few yards distant from the bobbing boat, I clearly saw a perfect mini-Atlantis rise out of the sparkly sea. Pebble-strewn, barnacled, and hairy with sea moss, the islet sank again, and only then was recognized as the back of a migrating whale. The magical whale-island was a true miracle, but the true monster was the doormat.

In any contest between monster and man I am of course on the side of the monster, and I was at first much bothered by reports of the jumbo, superscientific stakeout on the shores of Loch Ness. Two hundred volunteers working in relays have been searching for the fabled sea serpent with helicopters and telephoto movie cameras synchronized to operate six feet apart. (Loch Ness is twenty-four miles long and deep enough in spots to submerge New York's Pan Am Building, quite a monster in its own right.) Whether boat or cormorant, trout rising or dragonfly settling, record is being kept of all that moves on the loch. Film is sent for interpretation to the Ministry of Defence's Joint Air Reconnaissance Centre, the same outfit which once pinpointed Hitler's secret V-2-rocket launching station at Peenemünde.

If my theory is right, this is no way to catch a monster, so I was delighted to hear that under the assault of rampant technology Scotland's sea serpent is more than holding its own. Since the search began, nor coil nor scale nor inky fin has once troubled the murk-brown waters of the loch.

Mankind still has monsters, of course. The trouble is that they are no longer mythological. Rather, they are the terrifying things man creates with his technology and then cannot control—things like Peenemünde; things like smog, that foul thousand-mile blob visible from any jet; things like the cataclysmic, coiling, deadly dragon that is Vietnam.

Contemplating these things, we cannot but take delight in the Lady Sasquatch—and the brave Lochinvar in Loch Ness. If only they could meet and mate! Let us honor their skill at hide-and-seek. They must elude us. Escaping, they validate themselves. If the Abominable Snowman had been found, we would probably have him lugging packs up Everest by now.

The Loony Humor of the Yippies

🌸

My life is a game of multiple choice. People are not ugly or beautiful, fat or thin. They are always young, middle-aged, or old, tall, medium, or short, the middle-aged and the medium-height being appreciated least. So much for my own law of the excluded middle.

Can this old three-way habit explain my strange new fondness for yippies? Yippies! You mean those hairy-heads with dirty words painted on their foreheads? The people who nominated a pig for President? Well, yes. As I view the antics of today's far-out fringe, the flower children look appealingly sad, and plain old hippies have become a bore, but the yippies are really getting through. They make me laugh, and I like them.

I liked their inspired invasion of suburbia, the so-called cultural exchange program in which a rag-taggle crew from the East Village hired a sightseeing bus and toured Queens, gravely waggling their beards and aiming Instamatics at such strange sights as lawn sprinklers and housewives. I enjoyed their loony assault on the ROTC, the time they staged their own impromptu, somersaulting drill right alongside some hapless cadets. When the cadets were ordered to race fireman-fashion, each runner carrying another cadet on his back, the

October 1968

yips hoisted their girl friends piggyback and romped off with first, second, third, and fifth place. Best of all was the yippie who answered a subpoena to appear before the House Un-American Activities Committee wearing a red, white, and blue shirt with stars up one sleeve and stripes down the other. When he was arrested on the Capitol grounds—a law signed in July by President Johnson forbids "mutilation of the flag"— and the police officers in their patriotic frenzy tore the offending garment right off his impudent back, unwittingly they unveiled the blue and red Vietcong banner painted right on his skin.

It is pleasant to imagine this fellow by dawn's early light vesting himself for the big occasion. Naked and freshly warpainted by his loving wife (he *has* a loving wife, by the way; it was she who found the Yankee Doodle outfit on sale in a costume shop), he sits cross-legged on the floor of their pad, delicately nicking at his star-spangled seams with a rusty razor.

Savor his wicked glee. People who infer patriotism from haberdashery are ripe for ridicule. They are kindred spirits to the thousands of baseball fans who booed the "soul" "Star-Spangled Banner" of the blind folk singer José Feliciano. His song may have been the single interesting event of the 1968 World Series.

Of course not all the yippie pranks are funny. Nominating a pig for President never struck me as much of a joke. But then neither does the idea of waiting for a big-breasted girl to come out of the subway, the pastime that has lately convulsed mobs of Wall Streeters. But even when the yippies' sense of invention flags, I still admire their energy and follow-through, rare traits in the other strata of bead-and-sandal culture. It is one thing to dream up the President Pigasus idea, and quite another to go out and find a live pig, to notify the police and the press, to stage the parade, and even to lay in ham sandwiches to be passed out as campaign favors. Indeed, yippie stick-to-itiveness (would they mind that dear old term?) may be the most American thing about them.

(50

The other night, at the Yale University premiere of an avant-garde play in which the actors strip to loincloths and invite the audience to join in, all hands marched out into the streets afterward and promptly were arrested for indecent exposure. One hears the authentic sound of 1968 in the comment of New Haven's police chief: "As far as we're concerned, art stops at the door of the theater. Then we apply community standards."

A question the yippies raise is not where the art stops, but where the fun stops. Not long ago I came across a yippie guidebook on how to live for free in New York City. Free food. Free clothes. Free lodgings. Free legal advice—it's all there, all practical, and very funny reading. Free food becomes a matter of turning up at the big wholesale markets at the right midnight hours. And there are refinements: free cooking lessons (from the N.Y.C. Department of Markets); free buffaloes (from the U.S. Department of the Interior); free booze. This section ends: "The sun is free. Hair is free. Naked bodies are free. Smiles are free. Rain is free. Unfortunately there is no free air in New York. Con Edison's phone number is 679-6700."

The name of this work, alas . . . (Alas, or do I really mean huzzah? That is part of the problem of not quite knowing where the fun stops.) At any rate, the name of this work is *Hiccup the System*, or . . . . *the System*, the first word of the title being the same old four-letter one that you seem to run into everywhere nowadays: on the stage, in books, on the BBC, and painted on people's foreheads. Personally, I think usage of the word has gone completely amok (to employ one of my own four-letter favorites), and I side with Art Buchwald, who laments the now ubiquitous use of blunt Anglo-Saxon specifics in place of the quaint old four-letter, or rather four-dot, word: ". . . .". All the other euphemisms contain too much snigger for my taste, but ". . . ." by virtue of its very blankness invites the reader's own imagination, and I do hope that, like lipstick and the high-heeled shoe, ". . . ." is only temporarily out of fashion.

The traditional four-letter word has its rightful place too, and while I don't enjoy meeting it on cocktail napkins, one right place is probably in the title of the yippies' booklet, where it expresses the very essence of antisystemism and at the same time guards against book-of-the-month engulfment, or other contamination by the square world. Thousands of copies of *Fuck the System* have now been snatched up by schoolboys, dowagers, ministers, and even a baffled movie tycoon who wanted to buy the rights for a musical. He couldn't, of course. That was one of the best jokes of all. He couldn't buy it because it was free.

Irreverent obscenity and outrageous vulgarity are ancient and splendid weapons for social protest. Aristophanes had people flinging clods of manure around the stage, and there is much to ponder in the yippie with the four-letter word painted on his forehead who said, "After the napalming of children, nothing is obscene." Yippies, in truth, brim with moral outrage and are people capable of greater indignation than the most choleric congressman. Their crazy rags and dirty words are red flags to insist we take note of their passion.

Beyond all of that, the shaggy, painted, capering creatures have still another thing going for them. They seem to be the only group in this gloomy era of ours to be getting any fun out of it.

3

How It Seems and How It Is

A Message from Watts to Newark

❧

Now the Newark fires are out and the ugly postmortem has begun. But in all the acrid debate over what really touched the spark to Newark, the true beginning is being overlooked. The Newark riot really started in Watts. Watts was the turning point, a moment as significant in the long agony of American Negro history as John Brown's raid on Harpers Ferry. In a flash of flame in August of 1965, the forces of violence and of nonviolence were polarized. And traditional Negro passivity in the Northern ghettos came to an end.

Is it possible nobody got the message? It certainly looks that way this week in New Jersey. More disturbing yet, it looks that way in California too. Today, two years after the Watts riot—or the "revolt" as it is locally, and I think correctly, known—burnt-out Charcoal Alley still has not been rebuilt. Los Angeles still does not have a master plan. Nobody is even sure how many people live in Watts, let alone how much unemployment exists there. Is it 14 percent or 37 percent? Other numbers cling like burrs in your mind. Educationally, the area is 78 percent below the rest of the nation, including the South. Seventy-five percent of the population is under twenty-five years old. There is no new housing and no new industry. The area is so dangerously decayed that insurance is almost impossible to obtain. Chain stores have not reopened. Good jobs are five daily travel hours away. Of over $5 million

July 1967

channeled into Watts since the riots, 51 percent has gone for "administration." The ghetto has become a gigantic pork barrel, a place where antipoverty opportunists can get rich quick and split.

As Robert Kennedy told the Senate two weeks ago, federal antipoverty strategy has been "ineffective, inefficient, and degrading." His proposal to involve and rely on private enterprise by using tax incentives to lure job-producing plants into the ghettos is a good one, but its chances for passage are dim. And for every speech like Kennedy's, we seem to get another as irresponsible as Senator Percy's statement that he had canceled a Sunday morning visit to a Watts minister when told it would be "completely unsafe." This sort of nonsense undercuts all the patient efforts expended in Watts over the past two years to rebuild bridges between that shattered community and the rest of America.

I drove back to Watts last week to visit a friend of mine. He is a Yale law student named Stan Sanders, who has lived there all his life and is home this summer working on the antipoverty program. On the freeway I thought about the first time I had made this trip four years ago. Stan was a new friend then, and Watts was new to me, too—a peeling-stucco sprawl, not so much squalid as different, foreign, strange. Seeing again the crazy piles of auto junk, the stores hawking chitlings and greens, the strolling all-black throngs, I suddenly thought of the phrase used by medieval cartographers to identify unexplored territory. *Hic sunt leones*, they wrote. Here there are lions.

Stan runs a job-training program, and he had suggested I meet him at its headquarters in an empty storefront. Young men and women stood quietly in long queues. Many wore their hair in the natural, unstraightened style. You did not see that in Watts four years ago. How many other things had changed too. How simple Selma seemed in retrospect, how clear-cut the distinction there between good guys and bad guys, compared to the shifting ambiguities of Charcoal Alley.

(56

Stan bounded into the room, looking fit but harried, and led me to a rear office to meet a co-worker named Ocie Pastard. Ocie has the distinction of being one of the very few antipoverty workers still in Watts who was ·active there before August 1965, but he told me he plans to quit. Ocie is disillusioned. He believes the antipoverty program is not "sincere." "The money is just giving us something to play with over the summer, to keep us out of trouble," he says.

I asked what visible changes he saw. "Well," he said, "we got a whole bunch of yellow garbage cans. We got Christmas angels on the light poles. We got a genuine prefab asbestos Bureau of Public Assistance building. And we got a whole new kind of Uncle Tom. They don't scratch their heads. Sometimes they might even be quite militant. Sometimes they might relate quite well with the people. But all the time they sell 'em out when they get into a room."

Later Stan and I took a brief tour. Success Street is still unpaved, and men still sit and drink wine in the sun. Watts now does have a health clinic, a water and power company office, and a local branch of the state employment service. The people of Watts have a new pride in being black, an emergent sense of their own identity born in the flames of August 1965. As Stan wrote me from Yale, "the riots colored my conduct here more than any other single fact. It is against them that I measure the significance of my law school education."

Back at the Sanders house, I greeted Stan's seventy-two-year-old father, Hayes, and Phyllis, Stan's young wife, who is spending her first summer in Watts. "You don't believe this place until you lie in bed at night and listen," she said. "We hear sirens at least three or four times a night. Then all the dogs start up. Then you can hear all the kids come pouring out into the streets to see what's going on."

After the 1965 riots, Hayes Sanders was one of twenty-two Los Angeles citizens appointed to help allocate $5 million in antipoverty funds. He quit because "we passed a lot of resolutions, but I never could see no evidence of it. The only money

I ever saw was the ten cents a mile they gave me to drive back and forth to City Hall."

"Maybe you don't see any change," Stan said, "but people's attitudes here have changed—it's just not the same Watts."

That is the trouble. It is not the same Watts. And now it is not the same Newark, either. But it is still the same Los Angeles. I felt this but I did not say it, preferring to listen as Stan continued to talk:

"I don't actually know *what* to do with the kids on our payroll. It's impossible to train anybody in nine weeks. In that sense, Ocie is right. He claims that what we're really doing is fooling our own people, betraying them. He says the next time they burn anybody down here, what they ought to do is burn us."

Dumb Broad at a Dumb Fight

❧

ALTHOUGH until last week I had never personally attended a prizefight, I knew what I expected to see. The boxers' glistening, circling bodies and the hoarse roar of the crowd had become thoroughly familiar to me through years of exposure to Hollywood fight movies. The overall crummy ambiance of the sport and many vivid details—precise body patterns of trickling sweat, the blurry flash of mouthpiece, the slapping sound of leather on flesh—had all been shown me many times in much-magnified, pore-by-pore movie close-ups. Still, when I went to Lewiston, Maine, to watch Sonny Liston and Cassius Clay battle for the heavyweight championship of the world, I was worried. It wasn't the prospect of bloodshed that scared me, but the fear that despite years of slavish attention to Hollywood boxing movies, I might not really understand what was going on. I was afraid that when I was really seated at last at ringside, the lights glaring, my heart pounding, I might through ignorance fail to experience the primal sense of human combat that makes the rest of the sleazy game worthwhile.

When I watch a real fight on TV, I have great difficulty following or indeed even seeing the rapid-fire right-to-the-body, left-to-the-jaw activities that appear to be so obvious to the announcer and the roaring fans. By the time I can figure

June 1965

out whose right and left is which, everything has turned around. I desperately did not want this to happen when I was sitting at ringside. And since my very first fight was to be not only for the heavyweight title, but also Act II of a classic ring drama unequaled since the *Nibelungenlied*, I felt especially obliged both to comprehend and to savor the spectacle. I had no inkling then that my first fight would be boxing's last.

From the moment I landed in Maine two days before the fight until the evening of the battle itself, I always felt I was in *some* movie, but I was never sure which one. The turreted, broken-down old Poland Spring House Hotel, with its endless, tilted corridors and fretwork verandas fogged with cigar smoke, looked like a Charles Addams version of *Marienbad*. The crowds of beefy, sport-shirted fight fans, on the other hand, looked straight out of Warner Brothers' casting department. But among them I readily recognized some old newsreel faces. The stiff-limbed old man in the rocker was surely Jim Braddock, and there was Joe Walcott, in a cretonne chair, genially cuddling a small boy. Of course, I always knew who I was: the Dumb Broad at her first fight, asking silly questions.

I asked a sharply dressed veteran sportswriter what I should watch for, and he rasped, "It's all a big carnival, honey. Just take your position on the Ferris wheel and wave your balloon."

After the big press buildup of sinister bodyguards and Muslim assassins, I expected to find an Oriental spy movie atmosphere at Muhammad Ali's camp. But at Clay's motel headquarters rock 'n' roll music blared from an open doorway, several of his sparring partners friskily frugged along balconies, and hordes of girls waited worshipfully in the grassy courtyard and surged forward shrieking each time the champion popped out of his room to caper and wave.

Sonji Roi, the champ's twenty-four-year-old bride, looked like a very pretty Oriental kitten right out of an Arabian Nights B movie. While Cassius clowned, she was busy dyeing a wiglet in the bathroom sink as part of her preparations for the next night's elaborate toilette. She had never seen a real prizefight either, she told me, but she wasn't the least worried about her husband getting hurt. "He won't get his nose mashed," she said. "He's too conscious of how he looks." Just then Clay himself pranced into the bathroom, glanced in the mirror, and said, "She's almost as pretty as me." Sonji beamed. As I left their royal suite, I saw a super cliché, a Stepin Fetchit type, spraddled in an old chair guarding the door, just like in a Will Rogers movie. And it *was* Stepin Fetchit.

When I got into the arena on fight night, I felt momentarily reassured. Lights were blazing, the cigar smoke was suffocating, a hoarse voice was announcing the preliminary fights, and the sweat gleamed on the young fighters' backs. Everything looked and smelled just the way it was supposed to.

My seat was a good one. I sat near Cassius's corner and next to Cus D'Amato, Floyd Patterson's ex-manager and, I knew from my reading, one of the wisest old men of boxing. I asked D'Amato what I should watch, and he said, "Watch everything, the most interesting thing will arrest your attention."

I took a good deal of comfort from sitting next to the old manager and swiftly came to regard him as the grizzled, kindly Casey Stengel of the fight game. "Do you feel the gentle excitement beginning to build?" he inquired politely when the preliminary bouts ended. I didn't yet, but perhaps that was because I'd just seen two clumsy men knocked flat in the first two rounds of their fights. Although their performance, I knew, bore small resemblance to Clay's slogan—"float like a butterfly, sting like a bee"—D'Amato by then had made me feel that I *would* know a butterfly when I saw one. "Boxing," he said, "is the only sport in the world where you don't have to know anything. Just watch."

What I watched next was singer Robert Goulet stumble past me to the ring muttering, "I can't remember the words." As a matter of fact, he didn't remember the words—"by the dawn's early night," his voice boomed out over the crowd—but I remember Goulet much better than I do Liston and Clay, perhaps because he spent a longer time in the ring.

As for the world's heavyweight championship match itself, all my worst fears were confirmed. I didn't see the punch, I didn't understand why Liston didn't get up, I didn't know what referee Walcott was doing, and I didn't understand why or how Clay had won. "What happened?" I asked D'Amato.

"Short right," he said unsatisfactorily and melted away into the disgruntled crowd. As I too drifted through the crowd at ringside, seeking answers, a final fight began. Directly behind me there was a mighty thud, and the evening's fourth warrior crashed to the mat, this one in thirty-five seconds of the first round.

I felt awfully depressed, but there was some solace in knowing that around the world millions of people who really understood boxing felt exactly the way I did.

It wasn't the fight game or even a movie that I'd been watching, but the sleaziest sort of carnival sideshow. The occasion most reminded me of one of those roadside freak shows one sees advertised along empty stretches of desert highway. The first sign says, "Monster alive—five miles." The second promises, "Man-eating beast—one mile." But when you finally get there and pay your dollar to look at the monster alive, all you see is a dead snake.

It's the Idea That Offends

ON the day that a handsome movie actor with no previous political experience became the favored candidate for governor of California, I was forced to concede that I am quite as capable of rank prejudice as the next person. All I need is the right subject.

The subject in question is not Ronald Reagan himself but the entire notion of electing movie stars to high public office. My feelings on this matter are like good coffee—hot, strong, clear, and black. I hate the idea. That Reagan might indeed become a good governor is conceivable but, in this view, irrelevant. Andy Devine was probably a marvelous mayor of Van Nuys. It's the idea itself that offends.

To suddenly uncover a dark and unreasonable side to one's own nature is not pleasant, and the morning after Reagan's overwhelming victory in the Republican primary found me in even worse psychic than political distress. Outwardly calm to the point of glumness, I inwardly seethed. Prejudiced?—*Me?* You bet.

Three weeks later I was still in this exacerbated state of mind when a promise of deliverance arrived by mail. It was an invitation to cover the giant victory rally and $100-a-plate dinner at which the statewide slate of Republican candidates would be presented to the party faithful. The central ornament of the evening would be an address by Richard Nixon.

July 1966

According to the program, Mr. Nixon would be introduced by Ronald Reagan, who would be introduced by Senator George Murphy, who would be introduced by Art Linkletter. A more complete smorgasbord of political and acting styles and types could scarcely be imagined, and I set off for the Los Angeles Sports Arena in high hopes that enlightenment, if not deliverance, was finally at hand.

In blue-lit darkness, long rows of banquet tables completely covered a football-field-sized floor, and three thousand pastry Napoleons, nestling on gold doilies, proclaimed "V in 66" in red, white, and blue icing. Along the sidelines a tremendous, multitiered, floodlit dais, crowned by a giant screaming eagle, handsomely displayed hundreds of minor candidates and wives. A proud and gala scene, and as the band crashed into "The Stars and Stripes Forever," and a hundred Reagan girls marched downfield waving huge flags, the showmanship was dazzling. So was the big team itself, which, in a positive blaze of self-confidence, now strode through the cheering throng and ascended the dais.

Seated side by side, genial Art Linkletter, dignified Senator Murphy, boyish Reagan, and beautiful Mrs. Reagan made a smashingly attractive foursome. In a crack that set the prevailing tone of the evening, Linkletter said, "We are a hundred percent behind Lady Bird's program for beautification. We want to put handsome Ronnie Reagan in the governor's mansion."

Senator Murphy glanced up and down the dais and exclaimed, "My goodness, isn't this a great team? In thirty years we've never had one that looked this good!" Only a bomb-wielding anarchist could possibly give him an argument. As the evening wore on, the impression grew that the candidates were as happily dazzled by their own splendid appearance as was everyone else.

Reagan's praise of the visiting Nixon was gracefully expressed, as well it might be. In that very morning's paper, Reagan had attempted to cleanse himself from any taint of

(64

Goldwaterism by saying that he preferred to run his California campaign without outside help. Nixon's praise of Reagan, on the other hand, was faintly embarrassing. Nixon is still a terrible actor, despite his years of experience, and at times he sticks himself with lines that would trouble even Dobie Gillis, as when he said of LBJ, "I don't think he comes over too good on TV, but that Ronnie Reagan—wow!"

Listening to the familiar flat voice, it occurred to me that this man's previous humiliations at the polls are attributable more plainly to bad acting than those of any other modern candidate. (Dewey and even Stevenson were victims of bad casting; with Nixon it was bad makeup.) A pair of full-page portraits in the evening's elegant souvenir program suggested that Nixon's fundamental misunderstanding of his own image has not really changed. Reagan looks rugged, crinkly-eyed, and—yes, gubernatorial. Nixon has had himself photographed through so many layers of cheesecloth that he not only looks younger than Reagan, he looks younger than Doris Day.

The person who looked most attractive to me during Nixon's speech was his wife, Pat. Not only was she extremely pretty with a new, shorter hairdo, but in contrast to the tensely smiling jaws of the smashing foursome on the other side of the podium, she looked relaxed, almost carefree. There are few more heartrending sights than the smile on the face of a candidate's wife, any candidate, and I was pleased that she was out of it, for the moment at least.

My worst moment came when Senator Murphy, carried away by the splendor of Candidate Reagan, said, "Even his nonexperience may be a blessing in disguise, because he will gather around him all the very best advisers." As a Californian, I did not feel reassured.

Indeed, as far as reassurance goes, the entire evening was something of a bust. Eighteen months ago I had been able to write that Ronald Reagan should not even be *cast* as a governor. That is no longer true. And my overall impression of Nixon's present image is that, if anything, it has been enhanced by his proximity to the "good" image of Handsome Ronnie—wow. If there is a political lesson to be drawn from that, I don't care to know what it is.

But if I did not lose my prejudice that night, I did at least get to know it better. There is no built-in reason why an actor should not be capable of becoming as good a public servant as, say, a haberdasher. What troubles me is not that movie stars run for office, but that they find it easy to get elected. It should be difficult. It should be difficult for millionaires, too.

My perspective was restored a few days later when I met the famed songwriter Ira Gershwin, who wrote the lyrics for the great 1931 political satire *Of Thee I Sing*. (The song-and-dance man in that show was George Murphy.) I told Mr. Gershwin about the big Republican show and confided to him my fears about how easy it seemed these days for an actor to get himself elected to high office. "Was it the same in your day?" I asked.

"It was much worse," Gershwin said. "It's a pity, my dear, that you never saw Warren G. Harding. There was a man who really looked like a President."

Culture's Big Superevent

🌸

PERHAPS the world premiere of *Antony and Cleopatra*, which took place recently in the new Metropolitan Opera House at Lincoln Center, actually was the single biggest theatrical event in all of human history. The evidence assembled beforehand was impressive: the biggest house, the fanciest trappings, the highest budget, the most careful planning, the most talented artists, the hardest work, the loftiest hopes, the loudest fanfare. By opening night, many of the people gathering for the big event on both sides of the great, gilded proscenium arch must have felt, as I did, slightly dizzy at the thought of what was about to come off—nothing less than the cultural superevent of the culture center of the culture capital of the civilized world.

That it didn't, quite, was almost a relief. I was glad to have evidence that art is as elusive as ever, and that artistic success remains exceedingly difficult to achieve, even with the grandest budget and greatest goodwill in the world. Still, I was not prepared either for the big event to be quite such a big mistake. There is no other word. Much of what went on was a truly operatic disaster. *Sitting* there was a lot like having a front-row seat at an earthquake.

One so rarely gets a chance to witness a theatrical catastrophe on anything like this scale, that the spectacle is fascinating, not depressing. One knows perfectly well that glorious

September 1966

evenings of opera will take place at the new Met, just as they did at the old. Meanwhile one is free to sift the debris of the debacle and muse on the elusive nature of art.

Every art and artifice I can think of—from architecture to maquillage—was involved in putting on the big night. Outsized effects were invariably sought and, on occasion, found. Lit up at night, the enormous arches-and-glass facade of the new building has the requisite flash. The Metropolitan Opera has always been two shows, and on opening night, the lobby show too was grand—a splendid tapestry of beautiful people elegantly dressed. The show on stage had great richness, as did Miss Leontyne Price's voice. Yet it was apparent before the first-act curtain descended that something fundamental had gone terribly wrong.

As usual, that old devil great expectations was at fault. Three years ago, Rudolf Bing had told people he wanted to open the new house with a new opera, and he had asked Pulitzer Prize-winning composer Samuel Barber to write it. Composer Barber then told people he would compose his opera especially for Miss Price's voice. Miss Price told people she would take a year off just to train and rehearse for the part. Her three favorite composers, she added, were Verdi, Mozart, and Samuel Barber. Samuel Barber! Architect Wallace K. Harrison told people he spent ten years and nearly $50 million designing an opera house that could do anything. And when director Franco Zeffirelli saw the place, he exclaimed, "What a house! I love gadgets, I love toys, and this house is a Cadillac!"

But the ticket-holder does not see the Cadillac. What he sees are acres of sets, miles of fabric, and tons of props. Zeffirelli mobs do not just come on stage, they hatch out of unfolding sphinxes and pyramids. One pities the principals amid all this spectacle. Poor Miss Price, imprisoned in her ponderous hairdo, looks alarmingly like an old photograph of Sitting Bull.

The catchword among the critics the next day was "overproduced." But was overproduction the real villain, I wondered. Did Zeffirelli overwhelm, or Samuel Barber under-whelm? *Antony and Cleopatra* is an exotic, erotic love story; how can a composer undertake to tell it without writing any love music, nor any real love scenes? The Met deliberately and knowingly commissioned a new American opera for the great occasion; its reasons were political, not artistic. That was perhaps a basic mistake. Another mistake was Barber's choice of a dramatic subject so at odds with his own musical style. In any case, Barber's music was monotonous, Miss Price's costumes were ridiculous, and in the two locations where I sat you couldn't always hear and you couldn't always see. Worst of all, you couldn't care less.

There was no involvement with what was happening on stage. The most emotional moment of the night was the audience's full-throated and optimistic singing of "The Star-Spangled Banner" that started the show. The most dramatic moment was Bing's intermission announcement that the orchestra strike had just been settled. And the liveliest moment was when a kicky, twitchy frieze of fifty press photographers, or *operazzi*, scrambled onstage to photograph the audience. Opera audiences are disaster-conditioned, and this one remained friendly and touchingly hopeful to the end. All night we wanted desperately to yell *"Bravo!"* But there was nothing much to yell bravo about. It was the coldest house I have ever heard.

"Only in a culture center . . ." I mused afterward to a friend. "Lincoln Center is what America produces instead of art," he replied, quoting the celebrated remark of drama critic Robert Brustein.

A week later I finally got my excuse to yell "Bravo!" I found it in the work of another culture critic, George P. Elliott, who believes that we Americans have turned toward art as the final justification of our society. Discussing the original philosophy behind the construction of Lincoln Center, he said, "It was felt that disseminating art might help fill the spiritual vacuum accompanying our material affluence." He is probably right, but the experience of *Antony and Cleopatra* and the Metropolitan Opera suggests that art stubbornly refuses to play the role we have assigned it. Hooray for that, I say. Bravo, art!

Overcuddle and Megalull

MODERN air travel is the one occasion I can think of when one is suspended simultaneously both in space and in time, and in the past year I have been so suspended for over 100,000 miles. Even so, my palms still do get wet sometimes on takeoff. But most of the time I hold onto the subliminal, crazy notion that we are really up there atop an enormously long and sturdy pole. As long as I cannot see under the belly of the aircraft, things are fine.

Nor do I worry much over "jet fatigue," the disruption of the body clock that we have lately read so much about in connection with the new plans for the supersonic transport. My well-practiced defense against this menace of air travel is to keep warm—never, never board a plane without scarf, gloves, and long sleeves—and to relax. Whatever relaxes you best, do it, take it, drink it, or think it. This ought to work even when we are whisked cross-country in two hours instead of five.

What does dismay me, however, is the bitter personal knowledge, accumulated through thousands of uncomfortable hours aloft, that though the supersonics are almost here, the really comfortable seat, the draft-free cabin, the rapid luggage unloader, and even the adequate napkin-buttonhole still elude the designers' grasp.

February 1967

The trouble is that the airlines try to be all things to all people. In their frantic competition for our favor, the big planes have become flying cocktail lounges, movie theaters, chapels, even kosher restaurants. In fact, the airlines seem particularly carried away by their proximity to the Almighty. Once, bucketing through a stomach-wrenching snowstorm over the Rockies, my storm-tossed breakfast tray arrived bearing a little card headed, "For those who want to say a table grace . . .," followed by suggestions for brief, silent prayers in assorted faiths. Another time my tray card said, "The Vatican has granted a special dispensation from the laws of abstinence for Catholics," managing to leave the impression that those unfortunate Catholics flying on other airlines were slightly less close to God.

The airlines should get rid of the flimflam—the personalized matches, the four-course meals, the folksy ear-shattering announcements, and the massive paper ephemera of menus, scorecards, maps, wine lists, stereo catalogs, scrolls, parchments, movie reviews, and so on.

And the shameful fuss about drinks and food! The old standby question, "coffee, tea, or milk?" has, on first-class international flights, turned into a new standby question of vodka, or red or white wine, or champagne, or beer, and/or brandy, or liqueur, and which liqueur. You must also choose among seven entrées and four salad dressings, between aisle seat and window seat, stereo and movie, and which movie, and even whether you want the steak well-done, medium, or rare—all of this to be weighed and discussed on the telephone as you are booking your ticket.

The give-and-take between the passenger and the airline of his choice has evolved into such a complex, unprecedented new kind of relationship that new words are needed to describe it. Terms like *overcuddle*, or perhaps *megalull*, come to mind. These states may be all right for the once-a-year flier, or the family vacationist. But something must be done for the habitual traveler, those people who, like me, must board a

(72

plane every few weeks and who have been conditioned to drowse at the red danger-flash of a seat belt sign, to salivate at the sight of a macadamia nut, to rouse at the thump of a landing gear. The airlines offer first class, tourist class, and—some—a middle class. Perhaps they should offer still another: Austerity Class.

A first-class international flight can become a Roman orgy of overcuddle, far more dangerous to the traveler than jet fatigue. I recently made two Los Angeles–Rome round trips in less than a month, and it was on the homeward leg of the second of these ordeals that the notion of Austerity Class sprung into my weary, wine-soaked brain. I took out a notebook and began to make lists. The new Austerity service would offer plain food and drink in plain, draft-free cabins. There would be no stereo or movies, but travelers would be free to admire the scenery from uncurtained windows. All personnel would be very, very *quiet*. There would be no over-amplified shouting in the terminal about "final boarding process," no treacly crescendos of Muzak as you step aboard. Pilots would not be permitted to say things like "Hi, folks," nor to describe their intended routes, nor to crack jokes, nor, unless it were absolutely necessary, to say anything at all. Personnel, especially stewardesses, would take diction and voice-placement lessons, in all languages.

I am five foot three and Austerity would accommodate my dimensions. Its seats would be as comfortable for a woman of my height as for a six-foot-three man. She would not have to prop her back with one pillow, put another on her lap to raise her book to reading height, and a third behind her shoulders to ward off drafts. In fact, since there would *be* no drafts, she would not always have to lug on board an extra scarf and sweaters with long sleeves. For the heavy things she *must* carry, rolling carts would be provided between plane and ramp and down those long, long tunnels. There would be daylight windows in the washrooms. There would even be a decent buttonhole in the napkin, large enough to encompass a woman's suit button as well as a man's shirt button, thus granting her an even chance with the men of ending her flight with a gravy-free lap.

With these things supplied, a plane ride would be able to provide the things it does best: freedom from phones and friends, and a rare opportunity for the busy traveler to doze, to read, or just to reflect. A plane is a good place to write letters, too, though one must be careful what one commits to paper at such dizzying altitudes.

A plane, if you're traveling alone, is also a good place to be melancholy. Just as when you are driving a car at night, it offers an opportunity to let go a little, yet not too far. A plane is a bad place for an all-out sleep, but a good place to begin rest and recovery from the trip to the faraway places you've been, a decompression chamber between Here and There. Though a plane is not the ideal place really to think, to reassess or re-evaluate things, it is great place to have the illusion of doing so, and often the illusion will suffice.

As you sit flanneled in your lap robe, packed gently in your two or even three small pillows, toasted in your socks, and blinkered in your eyeshade—a long plane ride is a fine time to take stock, to dream a little, to sort out your ragbag mind, and decompress like a diver rising from the deeps.

Report from Underground

🌸

THE other night I infiltrated a crowd of 350 cultivated New York sophisticates who were squeezed into a dark cellar staring at a wrinkled bedsheet. The occasion was the world premiere of *Harlot*, yet another in the rash of "underground movies" which have become the current passion of New York's avant-garde. Word of the aesthetic uproar the underground movie craze has stirred up for the past year had finally reached us out in Hollywood, and I had come East to see if my hometown film industry has anything to worry about. I think we do: If a bunch of intelligent people will spend two solid hours and $2.50 apiece to see a single, grainy, wobbly shot projected onto a bedsheet of a man dressed up as Jean Harlow eating a banana (that's what we saw in the cellar), then the movie business must be in worse shape than anyone has any idea.

Pop artist Andy Warhol, who made *Harlot*, is as successful these days with his movies as he was when he was painting giant Campbell's soup cans on canvas and selling them at around $1,500 a throw. New York's top experimental-film prize has just been awarded to five of his 16-mm films, including *Sleep*, a six-and-a-half-hour inspection of a naked man asleep on a couch. Now august museums like the Metropolitan and the Carnegie are running special screenings of his and other underground film-makers' work. The Ford Foundation

January 1965

has handed out grants to twelve experimental film-makers, and soon a New York theater will be holding regular weekly screenings.

Movies like *Harlot* are called "underground" because until recently you couldn't see them anyplace. They are the home movies of the Pop underworld, turned out for their own deadpan amusement by the same droll folk who make sculpture out of auto wrecks, symphonies out of dishpans, and top-less bathing suits. It is so easy, and profitable, to be a Pop artist right now that I often feel the Mona Lisa smile is on the face of the painter, not the painting.

When I came to New York, my first stop was Warhol's studio, a place widely admired in avant-garde circles for its "crummy ambiance" of soup cans, comic books, and barbells. The artist, a soft-spoken young man who resembles an elfin meatcutter, graciously explained that since his films tend to be rather long, he had prepared a little sampler of his work. I saw one reel of *Eat*, a close-up of a man languidly nibbling a mush-room, and one of *Empire*, which is a single, motionless, sound-less, interminable shot of the lighted tip of the Empire State Building. In its entirety, *Empire* runs eight hours, but Warhol himself has never bothered to sit through it. Underground movies are made for the kicks of making them, and I suspect that, before the critics got in the act, and called them art, the same was true of the soup cans.

Though it was Warhol who urged me to attend the *Harlot* premiere that evening, the painter himself was too smart to waste the time. So after watching the star nibble his or her way through three or four bananas, I left, feeling confident that the picture's message had reached me loud and clear. The joke was a droll one, but not very. It had the fleeting charm of a bright saying lisped by someone else's child. And though both the film and the audience had been silent, a sort of sub-liminal snigger could be heard. I couldn't tell which side of the screen it was coming from, though, and I still wasn't quite sure whom the joke was on.

Not all underground movies are Pop Art, of course. The genre shades off slightly toward folk art at one end of the scale, and heavily toward arty pornography on the other. The best movie I saw was a wildly turbulent animated cartoon made by David Wise, a nine-year-old boy. David, "the Mozart of the underground cinema," began work on his film when he was six, and it is full of crayoned rocket crashes, *blams*, and *kazooms!* It has a marvelous sound track made by whirling his mother's eggbeater in a steel mixing bowl, and recently it won a prize at the Prague Film Festival.

It was depressing to go from David's exuberant workshop to a private screening of the most notorious of the underground movies, *Flaming Creatures*. This one is a languid transvestite orgy recently celebrated by Susan Sontag in *The Nation* as "a feast for open eyes." The current film catalog description notes: "*Flaming Creatures* will not be shown theatrically because our social-moral guides are sick. That's why Lenny Bruce cried at Idlewild Airport. This movie will be called a pornographic, degenerate, homosexual, trite, disgusting, etc., home movie." It is also sloppily made and ineffably sad, and I was glad when it was over.

As the lights came on, I knew at last whom the joke was on. It was on Mrs. Grundy. That redoubtable lady is finally dead. She was killed by the Supreme Court when it decided that to be branded "pornographic" a work must be without redeeming social importance or value. This qualification has made pornography so difficult for Mrs. Grundy-minded prosecutors to prove that now practically any work can find legal shelter under the wide umbrella of the First Amendment.

Even *Flaming Creatures* probably could be shown today. Another steamy and much-banned offering called *Scorpio Rising* has been doing smash business in Los Angeles ever since the Supreme Court ruling was invoked on its behalf. *Scorpio* is a loving, lurid look at the magenta and black-leather underworld of motorcycle cultists. Having sat through the thing twice, I doubt that *Scorpio* is any more sinister than a Debbie

Reynolds movie. I also doubt that it has one bit more social value even though, for me, *Scorpio* is even duller than Debbie to endure.

But the fact that, in the very same week last spring that *Scorpio* was banned, it earned the man who made it one of the coveted Ford Foundation grants seems to me a neat example of the total disarray in which our old standards of obscenity, public decency, and art all find themselves today. On the plane back to Hollywood from New York, for example, half a dozen passengers were reading *Candy*. (My hero was the man across the aisle who was reading *Candy*, listening to stereo on his earphones, watching the movie, and eating his lunch at the same time.) Despite the disclaimers, *Candy* is, of course, not only a satire on dirty books; it is deliberate pornography too. I cannot get too worked up about the matter; pornography never corrupted anybody. But I do wish that—now that Mrs. Grundy is dead—someone else could be found to take her place. A truly modern guardian of morals, she would have the job of keeping a clear and level eye on fake artists, phony art, and pompous, pretentious critics. Eternally vigilant, she would be especially wary any time she saw a home movie camera and a Mona Lisa smile on any artist older than a nine-year-old boy.

4

The Twentieth Century Is Dangerously Out of Human Scale

Flags in the Rain

WHENEVER a great man dies, when the solemn ceremony in black begins and a National Day of Mourning is declared, one wants to feel a part of it, one discovers a human need to hook in. Sometimes this is difficult to do. It was difficult for me last week because, like so many other Americans, I really had no strong emotions about the general and President who died at last in Washington. Though willing and even wanting to mourn, I had nothing from which to make my mourning gown.

This gentle death was so unlike the death in Dallas, the anguish in Memphis, or the confirmation brought home by Bobby that nightmare was loose in the land. Yet so many of the forms were the same. Death was back among us, riding the headlines and blotting the tube, demanding respect, commanding attention.

I am old enough to remember Eisenhower at war, but not quite old enough to have been a part of his most glorious days. By the time he ran for President, I was old enough to vote for him but chose not to. I never even encountered him as a journalist. So although I felt sympathy for his family and respect for his passing, it was at best a thin and distant grief, nothing in the least personal.

Then by the merest chance I happened to be in Washington visiting friends when his coffin crossed my life in a disturbing

April 1969

way. After a difficult lunch on the Sunday of the funeral, I wanted a solitary walk. Hiking along, hands in pockets in the rain, thinking about myself and not at all about him, I crossed a park, passed the White House, continued on across a chilly meadow, saw the crowd, and remembered, and nudging through it, came to the police barriers just in time and in exactly the right spot to see the big hearse arrive and to watch the ceremonial transfer of its burden to the black caisson.

Hearse, caisson, riderless horse—they were all so familiar. TV has shown us four state funerals in five years, four deaths in living color, Kennedy, Hoover, MacArthur, Ike, and not a detail spared. The honor guard is getting better at it, I reflected idly as the young men moved in punctilious slow-motion military choreography toward hearse and horse, lifting, sidestepping, saluting, standing back. Or it may be that I am getting used to it. Either way, the sole astonishment for me this time was the sheet of plastic over the flag. Plastic is a fit cover for a grapefruit half, perhaps even for a general's hat. But not a general's casket.

Rain may spoil a parade but it decorates a cortege, and if there is ever a time when the flag should be wet, surely it is at the funeral of a great general who has served his country as President. When his body is returning at last to the earth, and the coffin that contains it, by his own request, is the standard military box, what is being protected from the rain?

Caisson and cortege headed toward the Capitol, and the Sunday crowd broke up to stroll quietly away in small family clusters. Sunshine broke through heavy clouds, making a dappled and deceiving light on the wet lawns, and far off my right some piled logs of a still-smoking campfire, doubtless left over from a Sunday picnic, looked oddly like a sleeping man.

But my thoughts stayed on the flag. All the other flags mourning at half-staff all over Washington are wet, I thought. The ever-flying flag on the Marine Memorial, which I have watched for hours through the picture window of my friends'

(82

apartment, knows night and day and dawn and dusk and every season of the year.

In this season Washington waits for its cherry blossoms. Schoolchildren are here on spring vacation, and my hotel is full of brushed, shining girls and combed boys, a little embarrassed in their new Easter clothes and looking, this week anyway, like the kids you used to see on *Saturday Evening Post* covers.

Eisenhower looked this way too. He lived the way people used to live and he died the way they used to die—gradually, in bed. His death was the way we thought death ought to be.

"You think that's a man on fire, don't you?" Suddenly I was aware of the woman walking beside me, looking backward through her harlequin glasses at the thing in the grass. "You think that's a man on fire," she repeated.

It had never occurred to me, even in my star-spangled daydream, that the shape was a man on fire, only that it might be a man sleeping next to a fire. But the strange tone of her question, and its overtone of immolation, turned me around. I walked back reluctantly toward the rising white pillar of smoke, knowing it could not be a man on fire because the people continued to walk on past it. I was within a few yards before I saw what the thing really was. The pillar of steam was gushing up out of a manhole cover, and the man, his knees drawn up, was lying on top of it, perhaps to keep warm. The funeral crowd flowed by him like salmon up a stream.

When I got back to my hotel room and flicked the TV switch, the same military guard of honor ballet was going on, having changed only plane and direction. The coffin was rising now, ascending the steps of the Capitol.

Inside the Rotunda all the familiar parchment faces were suspended one by one on the TV tube. Mamie looked most real. "Receive the benediction," a minister commanded. Directly behind him the lean, gray face of General Westmoreland hung.

83)

The honor guard reverently removed the plastic, winding it up in familiar little ceremonial triangles, before President Nixon began to speak. I knew that his emotions, unlike my own, must be very intense, but his eulogy in its rehearsed stiffness recalled a high school graduation speech. He quoted Ike's great 1945 Guildhall address. Ike had said, "I come from the heart of America," and I thought: But today the heart wears a plastic cover, and another man is left to sleep out in the rain. I made my mourning from that.

Tarnished Buttons

🌼

WHEN the first Air Force cadets finally land on the moon, they will probably feel right at home. Judging from the space comics I've read, the bleak moonscape looks a lot like the bare, jagged, snowswept setting of the Air Force Academy at Colorado Springs. Some of the huge glass and steel buildings have a weird, lunar beauty—especially the astonishing, wing-formed, aluminum chapel—but the thing that struck me most forcibly when I toured the campus last week is that the place is not in human scale.

The academy nests on a vast, wind-raked mesa that has Pikes Peak and a lot of other Rocky Mountains for a backdrop. In all this magnificence, the great, gleaming Air Force buildings look puny and flimsy, and people just disappear. The campus looks deserted, even in full swing. The only cadets I saw during my two-day visit were a distant single file of tiny, monkish figures in dark hoods silhouetted against the snow, but by that time I felt lucky to see a cadet at all.

Ever since the beginning of the cheating scandal that has now forced 105 cadets to resign, the most frosty and mysterious aspect of the affair has been the official Air Force attitude. The service will not discuss the matter at any level whatsoever. At one point, cadets were threatened with court-martial if they talked about it even to their own mothers. As I am a reporter, my own private entente with the Air Force, ham-

February 1965

mered out in three days' direct negotiation with the Pentagon, officially entitled me to hear a general description of the cadet honor code that has caused all the trouble, and to make a brief tour of the academy campus.

I flew to Colorado. My guide turned out to be a polite major who told me that the honor code forbids cadets to lie, cheat, or steal and requires them to inform on those who do. He also told me that the academy playing fields could accommodate fifteen simultaneous football games; that the academy chapel is 150 feet tall; and that the surrounding hills are full of deer, bobcat, and bear. I wondered how many football games could actually be played, now that twenty-nine players have been dismissed from the squad; whether there are any sudden openings in the chapel choir; and whether the hills now might also contain a sprinkling of courageous, desperate AWOL cadets. Such tantalizing reveries having been officially forbidden, my nice major could only smile. When I asked whether the honor code would permit a cadet to lie to his girl, the major said he would look it up when we got back to the public relations office.

By the time our tour of this icy, bleak, space-age wonderland ended, I had an awful urge to walk on the grass, or throw a snowball. After waiting another hour in the office to clear the official answer about the cadet's girl, the major said he would have to call me, so I stole a pencil and left. Back in the hotel, I tried to figure out some things about cheating for myself.

It seems to me that people cheat for three reasons: Either something else suddenly becomes more important than not cheating; or one's definition of honor changes, and cheating no longer matters; or one cheats as a deliberate protest against the system. In the past year, all three motivations seem to have hit the cadet wing.

Perhaps neither the cadets nor the Air Force have had a clear enough definition of what a cadet is supposed to be—student, soldier, walking Air Force recruiting-poster robot, or

(86

some weird hybrid of them all. This confusion appears to be at the heart of the so-called cheating scandal. As students, the cadets feel that they themselves have been cheated in their expectations of academy life. But to the extent that the cadets are soldiers, the Air Force should indeed feel miserably, mortally betrayed. If the cadets are robots, there is nothing to discuss because robots have no honor.

The strict cadet honor code that lies at the heart of the Air Force Academy system has raised an interesting debate. Critics of the code, especially parents of the 105 now-disgraced cadets, have complained bitterly that the system actually destroys integrity by forcing cadets to become stool pigeons and squeal on their comrades. I don't agree. Words like *squeal* and *informer* are criminal terms, appropriate only in a prison context where everything is viewed as us-against-them. In a self-policed brotherhood, this concept simply does not apply. A pilot who reports his copilot for drunkenness obviously is not squealing.

But I think that in its zeal to achieve the highest possible standards of honor, the Air Force has attempted to stretch its code much too far and too thin. (You can *not* lie to your girl turns out to be the official answer to my question; in fact you cannot even lie about brushing your teeth.) General McDermott, Dean of the Faculty at the academy, defends the rigidities of the Air Force code by arguing that honor is a more critical matter for military personnel than for civilians. His reasoning, I am left to believe, is that Air Force officers, not civilians, are the people who may one day have to push the nuclear buttons. I'm afraid I don't agree with the general, either. Why is honor more important for soldiers than for statesmen, say? And as for button-pushing, I prefer to believe that the military people themselves are our weapons, as well as being our defenders. In this sense, they do not push the buttons—they *are* the buttons—and I'm sorry to see them tarnished even faintly.

Despite the Air Force's fanatic secrecy about the boys

involved, it is now possible to paste various snippets of information together and form a crude hypothetical model of the typical tarnished, cheating cadet. He was a fairly good student, and he was either a member of an athletic team or else a close friend of an athlete. He was having a little more trouble than usual with one particular course, and he was mixed up about his own private interpretation of the honor code. Most important, I suspect, he was trying hard to maintain what the cadets admiringly call a no-sweat attitude. Under the extreme stresses of their pressurized, dehumanized environment, cadets like to pretend they are normal American college boys. But they are not. It is incongruous, and in at least 105 cases it became impossible, to maintain this no-sweat attitude in a sweatbox, even one constructed of magnificent sweeps of aluminum and glass.

In self-defense, the beleaguered Air Force has of late taken to stressing repeatedly the extreme high caliber of the wing. Still, I wonder how much maturity grows in these high-caliber young men *after* they join the wing. Certainly they carry enormous military and academic loads, and over the four years of study a vast amount of technical information is crammed into their heads. Yet in the wake of the cheating scandal, there appears to be much truth in the bitter comment made to me by a recent member of the wing. "They talk to you so much about taking in an eighteen-year-old boy and building a well-rounded, twenty-two-year-old man. I think they build a well-rounded, twenty-two-year-old boy."

Three Little Words to Mistrust

❦

No joy can quite equal the unexpected joy, the stumbled-upon good fortune, the silver lining that unfurls without warning out of the black rags of life's normal, everyday adversity. One of these surprise silver linings unfurled in San Francisco last week when I learned that thanks to the presence in that lovely city of a giant convention of meat-packers, there was not a hotel room to be had.

Bless you, meat-packers! Without you I might never have known the pleasure of not being able to get into a big modern American hotel. Without you, meat-packers, I would never have found my way to the small, unpretentious, old-fashioned hotel just across the Golden Gate. The corridors of my little hotel were pleasingly crooked, and its rooms, of many different sizes and shapes, were rather randomly furnished—here an old washstand, there a bit of Danish modern. But it had real windows to fling open and shut, and even heavy curtains to draw against the morning glare. The bathroom looked like a bathroom, not a hospital operating theater. The walls were thick, the bed was comfortable, the closet was large, and the hangers were not locked onto the clothes-poles as if to imply that the tenant was a hanger thief. If you wanted something you picked up the telephone—a real phone, not a jukebox console—and asked for it. Whatever it was, it arrived with reasonable speed, appropriately hot or cold, and best of all,

March 1967

delivered by someone who appeared to enjoy bringing it. The staff of the little hotel treated me as a human being, not as "the party in 1269." It seemed to be a place where everyone simply wanted to make me feel at home.

It is time to confess that I am not perhaps your average guest. I was raised in hotels. I was not much older than Eloise when our family moved into our first hotel homestead. Others followed. We stayed in each one for several years, and we children always came to regard the various members of the hotel staff—the Cockney bellboys, the Negro valet, the Irish maids, the Italian cigar store man, and the fat, whistling doorman—not only as special friends, but as remote relatives, members of what the anthropologists would call our "extended family group." It was a rich, even exotic existence for a ten-year-old, and I am saddened to contemplate the impersonal aridity into which hotel life has fallen today.

But it can still be great fun to be in a hotel, away for a time from home, dogs, cats, children, and phones. That's what happened to me in San Francisco. My small hotel merely provided me with a pleasant, relaxing place to stay, then left me alone to enjoy it. Not getting into a big hotel turned out to mean not having to feel oneself being relentlessly air-conditioned, Muzaked, plasticized, and sanitized against one's will, all the while being told that this torment is being inflicted for one's own good. Or to put the matter in hotelese, "for your convenience."

Travelers in America should learn automatically to mistrust those three little words, "for your convenience." I first caught on to them about a year ago while standing in a hotel shower. Between my feet I noticed a sign: "This bathtub mat is placed here for your convenience and protection and to make your stay with us more enjoyable." I am unable to draw enjoyment from a rectangle of wet rubber, nor did enjoyment ensue after reading the next sign, which said, "This alarm clock has been installed beside your bed for your convenience." On my breakfast tray stood a placard saying, "For your convenience

(90

please call room service when you are finished, and your tray will be picked up."

All this high-flown chivying is for somebody's convenience all right—the kitchen wants its tray back, the switchboard doesn't want to be bothered with wake-me-up calls—but it is scarcely for mine.

A neat trick for anyone enmeshed in the high life of the affluent society is to navigate a safe course through all the people who say they are trying to do you a favor. It is not only that the ripe aroma of anticipated commerce is so sniff-able on all those outstretched helping hands. It is also that what they offer I don't want.

What I want most in a hotel is the feeling that someone is trying to make me comfortable there, that I am a welcome stranger. Personally I prefer old hotels and European hotels, the kind that have high ceilings, rotating fans, wood-paneled lounges, cavernous dining rooms, verandas, odd-shaped bed-rooms, big wardrobes, down puffs, huge mirrors, openable windows, and bathrooms with giant tubs, pull-chain toilets, wide-rim porcelain sinks, and enormous, thick towels hanging on heated racks.

The modern American motel is a fine invention, too, a marvelous blending of informal comfort with overnight effi-ciency and unbeatable if one is traveling with small children. But please, motelkeepers, stop telling me how wonderful it all is; don't cover every square inch of Formica tabletop with those little paper paeans in praise of yourself; let me discover some of your delights for myself.

Some good ones I have discovered include the automatic room coffee maker (wonderful on mornings you have to make that 6:00 A.M. plane) and the individual room refrigerator. Bathroom phone extensions turn out to be great time-savers. And not new but indispensable is the well-tuned television set. In motels I watch with pleasure all sorts of shows I would not dream of viewing at home.

On the other hand, why must new hotels have doors with

three kinds of locks? Why must they serve the coffee in Hottles, imprison the jam and butter in plastic cubes, and put the cream in a little paper tube? Why must they fasten that paper strip across the toilet and wrap up the water tumblers in paper bags?

The most fiendish device I have encountered is the automatic bed. This is a sort of vibrating mattress, activated by dropping a quarter in a slot, which promises to put the weary traveler to instant, relaxing, healthful sleep. I should have known better, but that night curiosity and exhaustion overcame me, and I lay down and pushed the button. At once a high-pitched whine issued from beneath my pillow, and the bed went into shuddering, heaving spasms. Faintly seasick, I groped my way to the bathroom to make a cold compress. There I found a horrid square of thin, corrugated plastic paper folded inside a transparent plastic bag. Stamped on the bag were the words, "Your personal washcloth! This luxury washcloth, an exclusive textile product, is yours with our compliments. Take it with you in this bag, as a souvenir. You will like using it as an all-purpose wiping cloth."

I took it with me all right. It was a dreadful souvenir of everything a hotel should not be, all wrapped up in one neat little genuine plastic bag.

Miseries of Being Bookbound

❧

I DO not recall a more thrilling opening to any book than these lines with which Bertrand Russell, now ninety-four, begins his autobiography:

> Three passions, simple but overwhelmingly strong, have governed my life: the longing for love, the search for knowledge, and unbearable pity for the suffering of mankind. These passions, like great winds, have blown me hither and thither, in a wayward course, over a deep ocean of anguish, reaching to the very verge of despair.
>
> I have sought love, first, because it brings ecstasy—ecstasy so great that I would often have sacrificed all the rest of life for a few hours of this joy. I have sought it, next, because it relieves loneliness—that terrible loneliness in which one shivering consciousness looks over the rim of the world into the cold unfathomable lifeless abyss. I have sought it, finally, because in the union of love I have seen, in a mystic miniature, the prefiguring vision of the heaven that saints and poets have imagined. This is what I sought, and though it might seem too good for human life, this is what—at last—I have found.

Lord Russell's autobiography, which is about to be published in this country, tumbled without warning out of my

March 1967

mailbox three weeks ago. Since then it has been my constant companion, riding around with me in my car each day and sitting each night atop the tall bookstack beside my bed. We have flown to San Francisco and passed a snowy Sunday in Connecticut. But though we are seldom more than inches apart—the book has its own special nesting place in my bulging canvas briefcase—the melancholy truth is that in all this time we have not yet even reached page 40 together.

There never was time enough on earth to read all the marvelous things that writers have put down on paper, but there seems to be even less time today. Books, books, books, books. They pile up on the stairs, stand in stacks on bureaus and shelves and tables and chairs, heap my bed table, overflow to the floor, and flood out into the hall again, all of them half-read or merely dipped into or set aside unopened in vain hopes of future time. But for the moment they lie abandoned in various degrees of unreadness all over my house.

Among the current casualties are a two-volume work on the history and practice of magic; *The Italians;* some John Osborne plays; three novels from friends; 1,300 historical pages on the Crusades which I hauled unread over 31,000 miles of Southeast Asia; a new Iris Murdoch novel, bought because one of her earlier books, read in the hospital after an operation, made me laugh so hard the stitches broke; an erotic curiosity published in France (read but not altogether understood); several recent volumes of popularized anthropology, and the first and only novel by a long-dead friend, published in 1931 and now out of print. I took that one down off a high shelf in a surge of remembrance late one recent night and placed it in scoring position, but I have been too busy, or too scared perhaps, to open it ever since.

In one room of my house, glum, reproachful piles of unread Sunday newspapers and semiskimmed magazines loom beside and over my darkened television set. I haven't felt too guilty about these neglected middens of newsprint ever since a friend, who for years has been professionally required to read the entire Sunday *New York Times*, told me that there is only one way to do it in comfort. It must be wintertime, he says, and you must be in Atlantic City. Then you get your wife and yourself and some brandy and your Sunday *Times* all swaddled in blankets in a big hooded wicker Bath chair, and you pay somebody to wheel you very slowly for several hours up and down the deserted boardwalk.

A cross-country plane ride is a good place to tackle the Sunday *Times*, too, but one must be wary. Last Sunday I staggered onto a plane in New York with the *Times* under my arm, Bertrand Russell in my briefcase. By the time we landed in Los Angeles, I had indeed read the *Times*, but I had also torn out of it reviews of three books that it seemed essential to read at once.

When the three new books arrive from the bookseller, I will doubtless follow my old habit and start them out in the central reading area, which is my night table. From there they will slowly move centrifugally, at different speeds and different stages of unreadness, to the more peripheral reading places of the house, to languish finally on the remotest high shelves or, with better luck, to be pressed into the hands of friends who have more reading time than I do. Some friends, however, have begun to avoid me.

Bookbound as I am, I am still not in as sad shape as a historian friend who once piled up research books along her staircase until it was possible to get upstairs only by hugging the banister and walking up Indian file. Then she started stacking the books on windowsills, bureau tops, and the bedroom floor. Her devoted husband did not complain until the piles of books began rising, like Babylonian watchtowers, all over his side of their bed. What I envy my friend, in addition to her husband, is the sort of mind that works like a Xerox copier. She is able somehow to comprehend whole pages in a single glance, whereas my own mind rattles along, one line at a time, clacking like an old Western Union machine. Marshall

McLuhan probably explains all this, but he is another author whose books I haven't had time to read.

In desperation I have finally enrolled in a speed-reading course. The first session was held last night, and the first thing we did was to fill out a form that asked us to state our main objective in taking the course. I wrote "faster reading," and settled back to learn how. Two hours later it had been proved to me that I could skim and comprehend childishly simple short stories at a respectable rate of seven hundred to a thousand words a minute, and that with proper training far more fantastic reading speeds were possible. By flashing a series of short phrases onto a movie screen for only tiny fractions of a second, our instructors showed us that we were capable, neurologically at least, of reading thirty thousand words a minute. All this was a great morale booster, and I look forward to my second lesson next week. But, before leaving, I amended the answer on my questionnaire to "faster reading of trivia." I certainly don't want to read Bertrand Russell at thirty thousand words a minute, or even seven hundred. I just want to hear, and savor, everything he has to tell me, word by word by slow-moving wonderful word.

The Real Tourist Trap

❦

THE American tourist is in trouble. All kinds of people in high places are worried about him, beginning with Lyndon Johnson, who is worrying about what the tourist is doing to our balance-of-payments problem. The President seems to see the tourist as some kind of termite nibbling away at the economic foundations of the wealthiest nation on earth.

Accordingly, he has proposed a two-year ban on "nonessential" travel, a move which in turn threw the booming U.S. travel industry into its own $4 billion dither. The State Department appears to be awfully worried about tourists, too. But whereas its chief concern used to be the protection of the U.S. citizen while he is under foreign flags, it now seems to care most about the protection of its own foreign policy from attacks by free-swinging tourists like Stokely Carmichael.

I have become rather worried about tourists myself, but mine is the conservationist's approach. Instead of harrying, chivying, threatening with travel taxes, and otherwise cramping the tourist's style, I think we ought to coddle, cosset, encourage, advise, underwrite, and indemnify him in every possible way. Huge herds of vigorous, curious, open-eyed Americans freely roaming the world are, it seems to me, quite possibly a vital national resource today as at no other time in our history.

There are several reasons for this. First, we are, relatively

January 1968

speaking, still a new country. Compared to well-traveled Europeans, we have a lot of catching up to do. Second, we are isolated geographically. Most important, as the world's most powerful nation, it is important that we be also its least provincial. If the citizens of Andorra or Lapland don't get around much, it makes little difference to the rest of us. But a huge and powerful nation walled off behind barriers of its own or of others' devising may become dangerous today not only to itself, but to mankind. That is the situation with Red China.

Americans ought to be the best-traveled, most cosmopolitan people on earth, not only because experience of the world is desirable in its own right, but because as a people acquires a great concentration of power, worldliness becomes a moral imperative. Against the fiscal problem of balance of payments, Johnson ought to consider the balance of the American mind.

I have a much-traveled friend, urbane and liberal in other matters, but in discussions of U.S. foreign policy distinctly a yellow-peril man. "The Chinese hate us," I have often heard him say, "and in view of the history of the white man in Asia, I think they have every right to hate us. But if we don't contain China now, one day they're—just—going—to—start—walking."

The answer to this argument, I think, is not to build higher walls, set stricter controls, tighten the rules on travel. The answer, to continue my friend's metaphor, is for us to start walking, first. Ideally there should be unlimited travel permitted to all nations on earth and among all nations of the earth. I am for tourists of any and all kinds: sneakered and sport-shirted and funny-hatted; pants-suited and pajamaed and jet-setted; knapsacked and bearded; festooned with Instamatics and phrase books and goofy sunglasses; traveling scientists and schoolteachers and schoolchildren and trade missions; Peace Corpsmen, corps de ballet, opera companies, and symphony players, tennis players, footballers, junketeering congressmen, and highballers—all of them to be set wandering and peering

(98

Shana Alexander

and snooping and migrating and exploring and studying and just mooching all over the face of the globe.

I also want the permission of my government to travel to China, Cuba, Syria, North Vietnam, and all the other forbidden spots on our shrinking planet. I think that, especially in the jet age, the right to travel is a civil right and a human right which, except for health reasons, ought not be restricted in any way.

What gives the State Department a right to issue passports and regulate travel? We are citizens, not subjects.

About a year ago, the Supreme Court ruled that people could not be punished criminally for going to areas declared off limits by the State Department, inasmuch as Congress had never passed any legislation to this effect. Accordingly, all new passports carry this wording: "Travel to, in or through the listed areas or countries, or any other area or country subsequently designated by the Secretary of State, without a passport specifically validated for such travel, is grounds for revocation or cancellation of the passport, or denial of passport facilities. (Section 5174, Title 22, Code of Federal Regulations.)"

Title 22 of the Federal Code embraces all passport rules. Recently the U.S. Court of Appeals in the Staughton Lynd case said that the State Department cannot control a citizen's travel, but it can decide where he may or may not take his passport. In short, responsibility has been shifted from the man to the document, and to my ears Title 22 begins to sound disturbingly like Catch-22.

Downshifting now from high policy considerations to the prosaic terms of the President's proposed tourism ban, we are told that the Administration is considering "some form of penalty tax on travel." Whether the new tax is to be apportioned by the day, by the head, or by the plane or steamship ticket is still unclear. It is not even certain yet whether the government wishes really to restrict travel or just to limit the flow of U.S. dollars abroad. If the latter is the case, why not just put a ceiling on the amount of money an American tourist can spend, the way the United Kingdom has restricted traveling Britons for years? This scheme would conserve more than dollars. Not shopping for all those souvenirs for Aunt Minnie would mean an enormous saving in the two commodities most precious to every tourist—his time and his energy. As a friend of mine remarked when she tottered home, laden with gifts, at the end of her first trip abroad, "the whole world is Bloomingdale's!" This being so, why not let Bloomingdale's and the White House work out the balance of payments and leave the rest of us free to enjoy ourselves?

Or if penalties *must* be imposed, why not a scheme to insure that tourists really do get their money's worth, really do see something on their travels: a ten-dollar fine for anyone who insists on a Hilton hotel; a five-dollar fine for demanding catsup; a four-dollar rebate for every phrase a tourist bothers to learn in the native language. Everyone's *first* trip abroad, of course, should be tax-free.

With the White House, the State Department, the Congress, and the Treasury each having its own ax to grind, it is difficult to predict which form the new travel restrictions may take. For the time being I think U.S. passport holders—at this moment there are nearly ten million of us—are best advised to keep their travel documents up to date and their eyes open. Otherwise the real tourist trap of our era may become the tourist's own backyard.

What Is the Truth of the Picture?

❦

PERHAPS every war has had its own image—Brady's rotting Confederate soldier, the gassed doughboys of World War I, the naked Chinese baby in Shanghai, Capa's Spanish loyalist flinging out his rifle at the moment of death, the hill of corpses at Belsen, the mushroom cloud, Korea's frozen retreating marines. In our newest image of war, one man fires a bullet into the brains of another man in a Saigon street.

His face is square to the camera, squinched in its instant of death, distorted by the bullet's impact like a pilot's in a power dive. Inches from his ear the instrument of that death is gripped by the bare hand and arm of a taller man with turtle head. The killer is South Vietnam national police chief General Loan. The victim is identified only as an officer of the Vietcong.

The execution appeared on hundreds of front pages throughout the world; the AP says it is one of the best-known photographs of the war. NBC-TV had it, too, in moving pictures: The skinny captive, hands tied, face beaten, is marched between husky guards to the waiting policeman. Sudden bang. Commercial.

But still unknown, despite worldwide uproar and outcry, is the name of the nameless Vietnamese in the plaid shirt. Who was the man?

March 1968

The new bad news from Vietnam has shaken us all. The entire tree of American opinion about the war, its branches drooping and weeping with doves, hawks, eagles, owls, now shudders in the lash of the new firestorm. To understand and evaluate what is happening, we are told, we will have to wait for the smoke of battle to clear. While we wait, the execution picture lies on my desk, a metaphor of the larger war, nagging me with numberless small riddles of its own.

What is the truth of this picture? Did Loan perform for the cameras? Is the picture more real or less real than the famous photograph of the flag-raising at Iwo Jima, which was a setup, or rather, a restaging for the camera of an actual moment of war? But who can restage death?

Who was the man?

What is truth in this war? Here is a sentence of reportage from *The New York Times:* "A Vietcong sniper, posing as a refugee and firing at American soldiers from a university window, was shot to death yesterday by South Vietnamese policemen, also posing as refugees."

Is the real importance of the picture the fact that this act was committed by "our" side? Or is it that the picture was printed at all? Every publication that ran it received outraged letters deploring the display of horror for its own sake. But if we had been able to print early pictures of the Nazi destruction of the Jews, millions might have been saved. A print of some confiscated Japanese-made film of Hiroshima was recently returned to Tokyo after lying for more than twenty years in locked American archives. Our government would not and still will not allow us to look. It is considered too horrible. I hope the Japanese will show it.

Killers, too, ask questions. The smoking revolver still in his hand, Loan discovers U.S. newsmen behind him and says, "Many Americans have died recently. So have many of my best friends. Buddha will understand. Do you?"

Later the policeman's friend, Vice-President Ky, comments, "The foreign press made a lot of news about this death, but none of you wrote about the Vietcong. Why worry about one damned V.C. terrorist when they are killing thousands of Vietnamese officers, men and women and children?"

This last, I think, is the real Judas question, and it is dreadful to hear its shameful echo in so many of our own newspapers as an attempt to justify one man's brutal act.

What are the rules of war? What are the special rules of guerrilla war? What constitutes a terrorist? Are black pajamas a uniform? What is a patriot in a guerrilla war? What is a spy? Who are the Vietcong? Who is the "enemy" in South Vietnam? How can you tell friend from foe? Who was the man?

Eddie Adams, who took the still photograph, says his own hand and camera moved reflexively as he saw the policeman's hand raise the revolver. Camera and weapon fired together. Thirty-one years ago in Spain, Robert Capa also fired his camera reflexively, but Capa stalked the moment of death. Adams says his picture was an accident. Does this fact make the death even more meaningless?

Who was the man?

Will the sight of this senseless execution perhaps have a seed effect, something that may germinate in time into widespread revulsion against the war? Or have we already seen so much horror on TV that this incident is without impact? Do we somehow hold the subliminal notion that the figure in the plaid shirt will get up and walk away during the commercial?

But there are other pictures—a South Vietnamese officer carrying the body of his dead child; green gardens red with blood. Can horror be judged comparatively, or competitively?

The questions continue. Some are too obvious to linger over long. For example: Is this the sort of "freedom and justice" that over half a million Americans are in Vietnam to fight for? Is this what some eighteen thousand already have died to defend? Of course it is not. In any war, outrages occur. Through poor questions, as well as worthy ones, a sort of negative answer does emerge; one learns at least what the point of the picture is not. It is not that in the Orient life is cheap;

not that turtle-head is trigger-happy; not that accidents happen; not that war is hell.

A positive answer is far more elusive, but the one I am working on goes something like this: In this image of war we have two figures. We watch what man does to man, "the forked animal." The horror is to see two men, each man looking at the other, speaking the same language, each breathing and standing on his legs until one man extinguishes the other with only a slight pressure of one finger of his outstretched hand.

Perhaps it is merely sentimental to think of man as any more than forked animal, pipe of flesh, naked ape. But if man is noble too, his nobility exists in his relation to other men. His virtue is society. This picture, then, is most dreadful because it so outrages the human association.

The Abuses of Sweet Charity

🌺

SOMETHING flinty has been happening to my heart. I no longer feel compelled to buy Girl Scout cookies from the children staked out in front of my supermarket, and when pennies, plastic key rings, or even Easter seals turn up unbidden in my mailbox, I feel no guilt at dropping them in the wastebasket. I have not yet set fire to an orphanage or kicked a beggar downstairs, but I do invite the malevolence of the gods by tearing up Worthy Cause chain letters—three in the past month.

My protest is not of the anarchistic Vivien Kellems variety. I feel reasonably cheerful about paying my taxes, and even about making payments on the bank loan they made necessary. If LBJ isn't depressed by his tax loan, why should I mope? Heigh-ho. Nor am I thinking right now of all the ineffectual do-gooders or the pious con men who operate in the name of sweet charity, odious though both groups are. No, mine is a newly exacerbated sensitivity to perfectly legitimate philanthropic appeals. It is not charity but its abuses that I object to. Worthy Causes must suffer greatly as a consequence.

I would hesitate even to mention my churlish dislike of being so relentlessly solicited had I not just checked with city hall and learned that between six thousand and seven thousand separate groups are passing the hat here in Los Angeles this year, *all* of them worthy causes. Nationally, giving money

May 1965

away is a $10 billion annual business, and an almost unbelievable 75 percent of this figure is given by individuals, who then deduct it. Surely with all this going on there must be other women who feel torn, as I do, between the maudlin futility of being Lady Bountiful and the temptation to become Hard-Hearted Hannah.

What I dislike most about the way the $10 billion is garnered is the recurring feeling that I am being hustled. I automatically resist being trapped or tricked into a position where I cannot gracefully say no. One of the fund-raising practices that annoy me is the use of IBM-style pledge cards that note last year's donation and automatically demand more. Is failure to escalate a crime? Some appeals even brazenly state that they know what I can afford to give, having checked on my income. Others publish thick "blackmail books" listing the percentage of his income that each donor contributes. Shame is a dreadful cudgel. I am repelled by the exploitation of children, and by the shock value of disease. The cheap giveaways are particularly offensive in that they take unfair advantage of the fact that people don't like to accept something for nothing, even something they don't at all want. The day I received a St. Christopher medal and a Star of David in the same mail did not increase my faith in the Almighty.

Charity, guilt, gratitude, and self-service are so hopelessly intertwined that you can work yourself into pretty strange positions trying to sort it out. Lately I have felt honor-bound to tell the little girl at the market, "No cookies, thank you," in a loud, firm voice. An easier out is to point to your loaded shopping bag and lie, "I bought my cookies on the way in, dear," but this is evasion of the issue and confers no honor. I think it is equally shifty to buy a poppy from a veteran on a street corner, then *not* wear it to the office. Nor do you acquire points by changing your name, moving to a new house, or getting yourself an unlisted telephone number. Those are coward's ways. You must refuse the appeal point-blank, *mano a mano*, to earn points in the Scrooge league. (There is a certain panache, though no real commitment to hard-heartedness, in buying a big rubber stamp, as a friend of mine recently felt driven to do, and stamping all unsolicited mail: DECEASED—RETURN TO SENDER.)

Various uncharitable thoughts such as these have been building up in me ever since last Christmas, a season in which my heart can harden to a truly sclerotic degree. So finally, last week, I bore this flinty vital organ of mine to the office of a professional fund-raiser, dumped it in his lap, and sought a professional opinion.

He was brisk, realistic, and unnerving. "The trouble with most people's giving," he said, "is that it's emotional—and it shouldn't be." The professional fund-raiser, unemotional and hygienic as a dentist, starts by "rating his market." He figures out how much money an organization needs, and then matches it with a list of prospective donors, often aided by an anonymous committee of people who have a good idea of what everyone on the list is worth. Though I didn't much like the sound of this, he told me Benjamin Franklin thought it up two hundred years ago. Franklin's advice was, first, to approach the people you know will give; second, to call on those you think may give, making sure to show them the first list; "and, lastly, do not neglect those who you are sure will give nothing, for in some of them you may be mistaken." I said this sounded like a great system but, now that we have over six thousand national fund-raising campaigns a year, a bit grueling on group one.

"People must learn to plan their giving," the fund-raiser said.

I suppose my trouble is that I don't really want to plan, though I certainly don't want the government to do it all for me, either, through some sort of tax or deduction scheme. Few greater feelings exist in life than the kick one gets from impulsively mailing off a check to a worthy cause without being asked.

The professional fund-raiser left me feeling that in his field as in most, honest professionalism is preferable to amateurism, and especially where $10 billion is involved. He also convinced me that for all the hue and cry, most people do not give enough.

But my man earns his living by raising money, and I still wanted to talk to a seasoned amateur. The next morning I dropped by to see a wonderfully warmhearted friend who has long been our neighborhood's champion fund-raiser, doorbell-ringer, raffle-ticket-seller and all-around promoter of worthy causes, including the Girl Scouts. She was both a scout leader and a brilliant cookie-pusher in her time. "What do you really think about the way charity works in this country?" I asked.

"Oh, for a kettle of boiling oil!" she cried.

The Womanly Art of Self-Defense

🌷

BARRY Goldwater has been striving to make a campaign issue out of the fact that "our wives, all women, feel unsafe on our streets" these days, and it is certainly true that many women have lately been loading their handbags with every kind of weapon from hatpins to pepper pots. In New York City, a notoriously violent community, women are carrying, and using, illegal switchblade knives and guns, on the theory that it is better to be illegal than dead. Even in my own pleasant, suburban southern California neighborhood, the sale of hand-guns for ladies has risen sharply. But I don't have one.

My feeling about guns hasn't changed since the days when I was a working girl living in an especially sinister part of Manhattan. I am a lightweight five foot three and no good at self-defense. But then and now I would not have a gun in the house. My reason is simple: Guns kill people, and none of us is quite so civilized as he or she might wish. Everyone is part animal part of the time, a good thing except that the animal part is apt to be the part that grabs for the gun. Human emotions are murky and indefinite, but a gun is a terribly definite instrument.

I know a father of five who brags that although he keeps half a dozen loaded guns at home, there is no danger of an accident. His children have been trained from infancy to know that the guns are *always* loaded. It will be sad, but not

October 1964

illogical, if one night this man walks in his front door and one of those well-trained kids plugs him right between the eyes. Or as a battle-scarred husband recently reminded me, "Any man who keeps a gun in his bedroom takes a chance of getting shot by his wife."

Modern life is full of modern tragedy: Babies drown in swimming pools, planes crash, assassins strike. But I suspect that the crime rate, particularly of sexual attacks on women, is soaring far higher and faster in our imagination than it actually is in our cities.

The fantasy of the homicidal sex fiend seems an oddly Victorian sort of nightmare to be having today. The natural habitat of this fellow is not the American home but Shock Theater, or the state mental hospital. Sometimes the hospitals slip up and allow a known sex psychopath to roam the streets, as happened recently in New York City. But then the blame for the resultant tragedy lies with the state, not the man. Still, with plain sex as richly available as it is now, I suspect that the old-fashioned rapist, like the streetwalker, is a vanishing breed, a figment from a less murky and indefinite age.

"Don't you *dare* touch me!" a New York career girl I know shouted when she awoke one night and saw the man standing at her bedside with flashlight and gun. He grabbed her purse and fled. Later she learned from the police that many of his previous victims had been attacked sexually as well as robbed. One can conclude from this story that a woman whose home is broken into decreases her chances of becoming an innocent victim by not acting like one. Most assaults involve some small element of collusion on the lady's part, even if it is only the unconscious collusion of freezing in terror. As for the streets, after all, certain women have walked them in perfect safety for years. Man is not woman's natural enemy. Perhaps women who are afraid of men shouldn't go out at night.

Most women instinctively don't like guns. We don't want them around. As a result of this prejudice, some of us are charmingly ill-informed. So I stopped by our friendly neighborhood discount store to get some facts. The salesman at the firearms counter looked like a Marine D.I.

"For plinking, ma'am, or home defense?" he inquired politely when I told him I was thinking about buying a gun. After I explained my circumstances—husband sometimes out of town, small child in house—the salesman suggested either a .22 automatic with which, he assured me, I "could run a hemstitch right up anybody's gut," or a .25-caliber revolver which he said would make for slower but more accurate needlework. He placed the two ugly little black things on the glass counter top, $27.98 for either model.

Chickening fast, I said I'd heard that in California it is illegal to shoot a prowler, even if he is on your porch, or halfway through your door.

"It's against the law to get killed, too," the salesman explained patiently. "If there's time, you can fire a warning shot. But if he's already got one foot in the door, he isn't going to stop there. So shoot him first, then drag him inside, then wipe the blood up outside. After that, call the cops."

I was only momentarily horrified, then realized this was in part his stock patter, intended to calm nervous ladies. When I smiled, he abandoned his ironic sales spiel and said what he really thought. "Women with guns are idiots. Fortunately, only one woman in a hundred buys a gun, and only one in a hundred who buys it will ever use it, and only one woman in *that* hundred will ever hit anything with it."

The salesman turned out to know something about women, as well as guns. The lady who buys a gun is either feeling like Frankie in "Frankie and Johnnie," or else she is in the state of mind of Linus clutching his security blanket. Either way, she needs calming down. When she calms down she admits that although she does sometimes feel unsafe on the streets, she would feel a lot more unsafe in a world where it was legal to carry a gun in a handbag.

5

But I Like It Here

🌷　　🌷

🌷

Love Songs to the Carburetor

❦

THREE deuces, to me, meant something that beat two pair. Then last week I heard one of the nation's recent rock 'n' roll hits, "Little G.T.O.," which goes, "She's got three deuces and a four-speed and a three-eighty-nine." Translated, this turns out to be a passionate love song to a Pontiac. (G.T.O. stands for Gran Turismo, and the three deuces refer to her three adorable carburetors.)

Love songs to automobiles have evidently been around for a couple of years now, though the first one, "409," was primitive stuff by current standards. It went, "Giddy-yap, giddy-yap, giddy-yap, four-oh-nine," so it is possible I did hear it but mistook it for a love song to a horse. Anyhow, car songs originated right here in southern California, so I can only explain my own protracted ignorance of the genre by confessing a long-standing, un-American uninterest in both rock 'n' roll music and cars. The two subjects bore me equally. I dislike the hard sell.

But I like feeling out of things even less, so last weekend I took a cram course and learned that a 409 is a Chevrolet and that since it was written, an entire new Pop Art form has been born. The beat is Beatle, the lingo hot-rod, and the take staggering—more than two million car records already sold. I also met the handful of delightful and very rich California youngsters, age fifteen to twenty-four, who are sharing the

November 1964

loot. One of them told me, "If you're over twenty-six, you probably don't know what we're talking about." Touché. "But half the world is under twenty-six today." Ouch.

These dozen or so California kids not only write, perform, and market all the car songs, they even sing on one another's records. It's not that they lack the normal sharklike instincts of the music business. Their cameraderie is enforced because they are the only living beings who are capable of emitting the unique West Coast Sound (a technical term, as in *Liverpool Sound*) any successful car song must have. The sound is at once ear-splitting, monotonous, and contrapuntal, and the lyrics allegedly evoke laughter, longing, tears, blood, and narrative suspense—most of it maddeningly unintelligible to the over-twenty-six ear.

The sound itself evolved from "surfing music." The subculture that evolved with it would fascinate Margaret Mead. Consider the complex, aboriginal relationships existing between just three of the car-song groups—the Beach Boys (three brothers, a neighbor, and a cousin); Jan and Dean (two college student friends of the Beach Boys), and The Fantastic Baggys (we will get to *them* in a moment). The head Beach Boy, Brian Wilson, is also half of the writing team of Wilson and Roger Christian (aged twenty-four). Roger is also the ranking disc jockey on Los Angeles' largest rock 'n' roll radio station, which is not irrelevant. Says Wilson with reverence, "Roger is a real car nut—his normal speech is only 40 percent comprehensible. And he has a tremendous knack for rhyming things with carburetor."

Roger says that Wilson's real forte is his "grasp of the teen-age mind." Certainly it is not rhyming. One of Wilson's most memorable verses begins, "Well, she got her daddy's car and she cruised through the hamburger stand, now. Seems she forgot all about the library like she told her old man, now." But the lyricist concluded the above stanza with the title line, "She'll have fun, fun, fun 'til her daddy takes the T-bird away," and thereby sold over 800,000 records.

(116

Jan and Dean's sound is considered so perfectly West Coast that you can practically hear that they are tall and blond and have surfboards under their arms. By now they have had five top-ten singles in a row, including "Dead Man's Curve," the first car *crash* song, as well as the first comic car song, "Little Old Lady from Pasadena." Dean is known as the "father of the falsetto." Jan is a medical student and also a self-taught sound engineer who has learned to balance Dean's falsetto harmonies with drag-race pit noises, arcane lyrics, and a number of other weird elements so perfectly that it is impossible to make out what one is hearing. Jan does this deliberately because "if they can hear the words, they'll turn their radio down. We want them to turn it up. It sort of relieves a kid's anxiety if he can drown out his parents."

"Little Old Lady" (the inspiration for which came to Jan as he was listening to a lecture on geriatric diseases) has by now earned almost enough money to pay for his entire medical education. It has also spawned a splendidly baroque sequel, called the "Anaheim, Azusa, and Cucamonga Sewing Circle, Book Review and Timing Association," which represents the fullest flower of the car song to date. This one is about a bunch of little old ladies whose sewing circle is a front for a hot-car club. It kicks off with three bars of Bach's Chorale No. 54, transposed for barbershop harmony by Jan and sung by The Fantastic Baggys. Then it works up into a couplet that seems to say, "They run to their cars like the start at Le Mans, then go spinnin' doughnuts on their lawns," accompanied by full chamber orchestra. For a finish, the harpsichord rides it out while the Baggys fade off into the distance softly chanting, "Go, Granny, Go!"

A final word about baggies. Baggies are loose surfing shorts. The Fantastic Baggys (I think they are spelling their own name wrong) is a generic term for the apparent twelve-singer chorus that backs up Jan and Dean. But most of these voices are Jan and Dean themselves, electronically multiplied. Only two belong to the *real* Baggys, a couple of nineteen-year-olds before whose multiple identities my over-twenty-six mind boggles helplessly. As The Fantastic Baggys they have issued their own album, "Tell 'Em I'm Surfin'." They have also recorded as Philip and Stephen, which are their real names, though on that particular record they pretend to be an English group and sing with the Liverpool Sound. Then they are also known as the Streetcleaners, who sing something called, "That's Cool, That's Trash," which they also composed.

When I last saw the Baggys, they were hard at work in a tiny Hollywood recording studio teaching more of their compositions to four Mexican kids just off the bus from Ensenada. The session was rough going: The Mexicans spoke no English, the Baggys spoke no Spanish, and nobody in the room could read any music. But all hands seemed to feel the effort to communicate was worth it. "We've got the talent, and we're gonna instill it in these geniuses," the Baggys' manager explained to me. "We're making 'em into four Beatles with Spanish accents and calling 'em the Iguanas."

I wish the Iguanas well, and I'm very glad I took that cram course. Along with everything else, I was reminded that when you let yourself get bored too easily, you sure miss out on a lot of fun, fun, fun.

So Now I Own a Net Bikini

THANK God I am immune to high fashion at last. This year, for example, I haven't the slightest yen to own a leather suit, fur knickers, a djellaba, or a plastic space helmet. My immunity took years of exposure to fashion magazines to acquire. But having finally faced the fact that I am five foot three and comfortably over thirty, and do not live my life in a wind tunnel, a seraglio, or the African veldt, the wide variance between my own appearance and what I see in fashion photographs has ceased to trouble me. I continue to admire the professional fashion people for their great energy and virtuosity, but I also admire myself for resisting it.

It's not that I don't care how I look. It's just that I hate being told what to do. I resist being manipulated, especially by experts. I have never met a couturier I didn't like. But most professional fashion drumbeaters annoy me, and haughty saleswomen scare me to death. If I were really faced with the choice that high fashion now offers—that of dressing up as a Martian, a baby doll, or a houri—I would honestly rather be a frump.

Fortunately I don't have to choose, thanks to a little dressmaker whose name I would not dream of disclosing. I have always enjoyed making clothes myself, and I am inordinately fond of the few women with lint on their sleeves and pins in their mouths who still practice the art.

May 1965

But though I ceased to worry about looking fashionably well-dressed long ago, the problem of looking well-undressed grows worse each year. I have never felt so abandoned by the fashion industry as I did last week while I shopped for a new bathing suit. My beach needs are simple, and it is difficult to believe they are unique. I just want to blend harmoniously into the beachscape in reasonable comfort, which means to me a one-piece, one-color maillot, a classic style not usually hard to come by. No bikinis, thank you, no tank suits, no little-girl dirndls, no old-lady beach dresses, no sequins, no luminous paint, no tropical sarongs and, please, a minimum of hostile interior rubber and wire. These hidden armatures make me feel that an independent eighteen-year-old Amazon is sharing my suit.

Last week half the racks held bikinis, and the other half dripped enough black mesh, veiling, and fishnet to make me think a school of tattered mermaids had just molted there. These last were the so-called scandal suits—clinging black leotards from which huge hunks of side, front, or midsection have been sliced away and replaced by wide-mesh elastic net. They are the logical fashion evolution of last year's Pop Art masterpiece, the topless bathing suit, and they give the illusion of bareness, which is almost always better to look at than the real thing. As Yogi Bear would say, they are smarter than the average bare.

Mashed into a back corner I finally came upon a pitifully scant selection of maillots, chose a brown one, and slunk into a fitting room. Finding oneself alone at last with an untried bathing suit and a full-length mirror is always a tense moment. Looking down at the small puddle of fabric I was about to step into, I drew some absolutely absurd assurance from seeing the name of Jackie Kennedy's dress designer written on the tag. But indeed, the suit was very pleasant, and I bought it.

The next day, with a thirteen-year-old friend in tow, I headed for the beach, rather expecting the place to look like the big undersea number from the Lido show in Las Vegas.

But thank God, the beach is still the beach, the same old blinding blaze of sun, screams, sand, and sports—of which the greatest is still people-watching—and not a brass bed in sight.

My young friend and all her crowd surprised me by turning up in what they call "semibikinis"—two-piece suits with low-waisted pants—but I felt that, scandalwise, their firm brown tummies and the braces on their teeth canceled each other out. The papers reported over a million people on the beach that day, but I saw only one of the fishnet suits—the one with the big V from shoulder to navel. Our whole beach stared when the girl spread out her towel and lay down. But the only people who came by to make a closer inspection were a man walking a dog and another man who carried an infant on his shoulder. "You look very, very pretty," he told her, and she certainly did.

On Monday morning I telephoned Cole of California, which originated the new scandal suits, and learned to my astonishment that they are the biggest runaway sellers ever to hit the swimwear industry.

Cole expects to sell over 200,000 of them, has had to buy a new factory to produce them, and is rushing out with a follow-up collection in which the net is nude-color and the solid parts are patterned tiger, zebra, or leopard. To learn why they were so popular, Cole suggested I talk to Miss Margit Fellegi, a tiny Hungarian former ballerina who has been designing Cole bathing suits for twenty-eight years.

She was jubilant. "It's the fabric!" she cried, explaining that the new mesh, which she had invented after thirty years of experimentation, gives the figure-control of a girdle, yet is as transparent and flattering as a cancan girl's black net stockings. "Once we learned to sew holes, we knew we had it," she went on. "Now I can slice the body up any way I want to, and know that the solid pieces will hold together. If I want a very long leg line, I can start it at the armpit. I can make the lowest cut bra and you can't pop out. I can redesign the human body!"

121)

The moment was a lot like interviewing Archimedes just after his bath. Thinking about it later, I found my footsteps returning to the department store fitting room. Soon I was inside two pieces of black and white polka-dot fabric joined by a wide black mesh midriff. I stared into the mirror and decided—O vanity!—that the little Hungarian lady was absolutely right. "Of course at my age, if I did buy this thing, I would wear it only in my own backyard," I told the saleslady. And meant it.

"You're only as old as you feel, honey," she said haughtily.

"Charge and send," I replied.

So now I own a net bikini. I can wear it both for backyard sunbathing and for laughing up my nonexistent sleeve. The last real fashion story I reported concerned the topless bathing suit, which I called "fashion's best joke in years." If it has turned out that I may not be quite immune to fashion after all, at least I now know whom the joke is on.

Agent 008—Where Are You?

GIVE me my choice today between a glamorous secret agent with hair like a black comma and a spindle-shanked, dope-shooting misanthrope, and I will unhesitatingly choose the dope shooter. It is not that I am all that fond of Sherlock Holmes, but that I have become so bored with James Bond. I am well aware that I speak for a fast-dwindling minority of the earth's population. Bond, Secret Agent 007, or, to use his fine Italian handle, "Mr. Kiss-kiss, bang-bang," is the international superhero of modern times. The dozen or so Bond books by the late Ian Fleming have sold some 50 million copies in eleven languages; the three Bond movies are breaking all box-office records; TV is swarming with copycat Bond characters, and the worldwide avalanche of 007 merchandise includes everything from Bond-licensed bedsheets to a complete line of what is known, revoltingly, as "men's toiletries." In short, the Bond image is now so potent it even has the selling power to deodorize armpits.

In my opposition to it all, I stand almost alone, but not quite. The party organ of the East German government is with me; and so, oddly enough, are the Vatican newspaper, the intellectual British journal *New Statesman*, and Malcolm Muggeridge, ex-editor of *Punch*. Even for a Bond caper, we make strange bedfellows! My allies find Bond a unique blend of sex, snobbery, and sadism so nasty as to be "far more dangerous than

July 1965

straight pornography." I disagree. There is something wrong with Bond all right, but that is not it. He has simply become too dull.

That Bond is turning blah is not altogether Fleming's fault. As the writer often said, he never intended to be in the Shakespeare sweepstakes. "I am in the business," he always insisted, "of getting intelligent, uninhibited adolescents of all ages, in trains, aeroplanes, and beds, to turn over the page." Neatly put, as usual, and he certainly had my number. I first encountered his secret agent in 1961 at 3:30 in the morning on an Atlanta to Birmingham train journey of nightmarish discomfort; for sheer horror, the Paris–Orient express has nothing on the Southern Railroad! I was blinking and gasping for breath on the between-cars platform when another insomniac lady pressed a sooty copy of *Casino Royale* into my sweaty hand. Fleming's steel-nerved hero got me nicely through the rest of that awful night and, with the incalculable assistance of his great gallery of Dick Tracyish villains—Goldfinger, Dr. No, Hugo Drax, Blofeld—we all made it through many other bouts of sleeplessness or nocturnal boredom in months to come.

When the James Bond movies began to come out, I was eager to see how my evil old nocturnal pals would survive the journey from book to screen. Alas, not well. They had become caricatures of caricatures. Even Agent 007 had become the put-on's put-on, and once that mistake was made, no amount of rubberized monsters or pulsating Technicolor flesh could bring 'em back alive. The idea of burlesquing the books, rather than doing them straight, turns out to have come from Sean Connery himself. It was necessary, the actor told me when I met him last year, "because since Bond is a fantasy man and not a real man, we had to make him even less real on the screen." This is purest Hollywood logic, with which I long ago learned not to argue. When Fleming's first novel was bought by Hollywood, the producer ordered his screenwriters to convert it into what the industry calls a "starring vehicle" for a then minor actress, Capucine. Thereafter the writers, who are friends of mine, spent two frustrating years struggling to write James Bond out of *Casino Royale*. Though they had no better luck eradicating 007 than did SMERSH, they may have been better paid.

Still the remark about the fantasy man did explain my own growing boredom with Bond. For Bond is no ordinary figment; he is the bachelor fantasy of every married man's dream. Fleming himself confessed that he had invented 007 "as an antibody to my hysterical alarm at getting married at the age of forty-three." *Casino Royale* can be viewed as the first of a dozen long sensuous good-bye letters to all that can now never be, and possibly never was. Good stuff for male readers, but what woman can remain interested for long in the erotic daydreams of Walter Mitty? Not even Mrs. Mitty, I suspect.

Eventually the Bond books were weakened, too, by their enormous, unexpected success. As Fleming was forced to pump more and more hot air into each new fantasy balloon, the reader finally could not ignore the pathetic rasp of the writer gasping for breath. Bond eventually gets silly, and the reader begins yearning for someone as grittily real as, say, Philip Marlowe to come along. Amid all Bond's Miami-moderne finery, the Marlowe miasma of sweat and peeling stucco would seem positively invigorating. I also prefer Marlowe's attitude toward women. While unmistakably red-blooded, he could take them or leave them alone, and if they were too approachable, he was inclined to become less interested, not more.

When I realized that despite my own torpor, the world was going absolutely insane over *Goldfinger*—lines in front of some theaters by then were a half-mile long—I decided to go back for a second look. This time I invited my neighbor to come along. She is a sophisticated European woman and eager to see the movie her teen-aged, Americanized son and daughter were so worked up about. But to our mutual astonishment we soon found ourselves dozing over the popcorn.

125)

"All zat senseless banging, crashing, shooting—so boring!" she said when we woke up, and I helplessly agreed.

In his new book, *The James Bond Dossier*, novelist Kingsley Amis has computed that Bond "shoots, throttles, stabs, buries in guano, causes to be blown out of the broken window of a high-flying aircraft, or in some other way directly encompasses the deaths of thirty-eight-and-a-half bad men: He and a barracuda share responsibility for the death of a thirty-ninth." Amis considers actor Connery all wrong for the film part. Author Ian Fleming approved the actor, but ultimately was himself bored by his own character. He once said he found James Bond to be "an extremely dull, uninteresting man. . . . I wanted my hero to be almost an anonymous blunt instrument," he added.

For my taste, the author succeeded too well. My own hero, in contrast to Fleming's, would be rumpled, not slick; warm, not cold; flawed, not perfect; tarnished, not toiletried; honestly afraid, not idiotically brave; in short, man, not superman.

Don't Change a Hair for Me, Batman

❦

EVERY once in a while, an event occurs that seems so exquisitely right for its own time that one is left gasping at the infinite fitness of things, the perfection of the Grand Design. In a small way, such an event was the arrival last month of the new TV show *Batman*. I was far from alone in my admiration. Thanks to ear-splitting promotion, the show struck this country with the impact of a Hindu religious festival. Overnight it had the Number One TV rating; kids coast to coast were set wildly dancing the Batusi; big actors like Sinatra were reported squabbling over small parts; rival networks were frantically mocking up imitations, and of course the critics were sounding off in all directions, saying things like, "This show is so bad, it's good. If it were any better, it would be terrible."

Still, I would not normally have looked at *Batman*. My personal interest in television serials and comic books, never high, has by now been ground down into a dull, throbbing ache by the avalanche of "in" and "out" jokes, by High Camp and Low Camp, by Pop Art and Op Art, and particularly by all spoofs of James Bond. I especially mistrust spoofs of spoofs because in this bewildering form—as in the play-within-a-play —so much hokum and sheer chaff gets by under the excuse of *double entendre*.

February 1966

But one night, having idly curled up with a martini, I flicked on the TV set and—THWUCKK!!—*Batman* got to me like an arrow in the heart. There seemed to be something so absolutely right about the show. I liked seeing a comic strip come alive, yet not change a hair. Serious artist friends say that *Batman* really should be an animated cartoon, but I say that would spoil it. There is something about live (more or less) actors playing cartoon characters that delights me. The dynamic duo in their baggy underwear, the faint potbelly on Batman, the enormous size of the "boy," Robin, produce in me a small, quiet joy. There is something about this show that is like looking through a plain round hole at clear blue sky. Maybe the best word is transparency; whatever there is, it is not opaque, it is all there.

In short, I was charmed. It was surely not the gimmicky spoof-on-spoof of the batpoles, the batcave, or the batmobile that I loved, nor was it the campy animated "ZOWIE!"s that zoomed out of the screen. It was not any personal childhood identification with Robin, the Boy Wonder, nor indeed with any comic strip. The phantom heroes of my childhood were audible but never visible: the Green Hornet, the Lone Ranger, Wilma Deering. My own private dynamic duo was Commissioner Lewis J. Valentine and Colonel H. Norman Schwartzkopf. (Look it up.)

Another private delight was to meet once again the intense clarity and the rigid economy of comic-strip literary style. The locale of Batman is "Gotham City." The hero is "millionaire Bruce Wayne." No equivocation there. An elaborate, fantastical conveyor belt bears the infinitely reassuring sign: "Conveyor Belt." There are lightning-fast transitions: We watch a girl being hideously, fatally, irrevocably poisoned, and a split second later Batman says, "Don't move. I'll get the Universal Drug-Antidote!" There are preposterous jokes, riddles and codes, great anatomical villains—Joker, the Penguin, Clay-Face—and sweet expletives—Holy Alphabet! Holy Barracuda! By the time *Batman* was over, I had decided that it

(128

pleasantly parodied its own commercials, its own TV trailers, all other TV adventure series, all the old B movies—in short, television itself. Three cheers!

"Ah-haa, but will *Batman* hold up six weeks from now?" they whisper at the watering holes where the TV-makers gather. Probably not. The temptation to "improve" explosive success is almost irresistible. Already the second week's episode showed signs of deterioration. Its main trouble, I thought, was the villain, "the Penguin," dreadfully played by Burgess Meredith. He was so actorish he nearly ruined the show. Later I read an interview in which Meredith said he found the part an "interesting challenge." He added that to him, as a classic actor, King Lear suggested an aged lion, Falstaff an old bear. He said that he planned to "use birdlike characteristics without being overly stylized," and he even mentioned the "penguin-like waddle of Charlie Chaplin." Holy Actors Studio! Comic-strip artist Bob Kane, who originally invented the Penguin, says he got the idea off a pack of Kools.

Still, why should this whole silly thing hit me so hard? I don't think I would have liked *Batman* so much had I not just seen, in rapid succession, the following creative works in other fields: *Doctor Zhivago, Barney's Beanery,* and *The Persecution and Assassination of Jean-Paul Marat as Performed by the Inmates of the Asylum of Charenton under the Direction of the Marquis de Sade.* I was touted on *Zhivago,* or rather off it, by a trusted friend who telephoned me coast to coast simply to say, "I have just seen a marvelous movie which you will absolutely hate." Thus goaded into action, I slouched to the box office and saw one of the most beautiful movies ever made. Next I read that the Hollywood diner in which I have often had coffee, Barney's Beanery, has been reproduced by an avant-garde artist in plaster of Paris, complete with bacon smells, cooking sounds, and papier-mâché customers, and proclaimed a genuine twenty-two-foot-long, $25,000 work of art. Finally I saw *Marat/Sade,* a multileveled, many-dimensional play-within-a-play directed by England's most brilliant director, in which the well-schooled members of the Royal Shakespeare Company impersonate a tribe of grotesque eighteenth-century lunatics. The first shock of scabs, scars, and straitjackets wore off surprisingly quickly, and after that, gibber and drool as everybody might, I found my attention wandering. This exquisitely staged galumphing of gargoyles seemed very much like a high-class version of *Li'l Abner*. Compared to my present stifling, baffling aesthetic confusion, *Batman* is simple-minded—and irresistible.

Batman's success has everybody in show business busy analyzing why, and the answer may be that life and art are comic strips after all. *Batman*'s euphoric producer himself proclaims, "You know why our show's a hit? We get everybody. To the kids it's real, to the adults it's camp." But I'm not even sure of that anymore. The youngster I know who likes *Batman* best happens to be a pretty dumb kid, in the bottom quarter of his class, who watches the dynamic duo in a perfect frenzy of eye-rolling, yuck-yucking, and hearty, chucklesome pokes in the ribs. For *him* it's camp; for *me* it's real.

A Nonfictional Visit with Truman Capote

❧

I LOVE to read, and what I love to read most these days is high-style reportage. Over the years I have also become increasingly fond of poetry, biography, letters, and so on, while novels and short stories interest me less and less. This dwindling interest in what is "made up," and the growing appetite for what is "real," is something that happens to many readers and, I think, to some writers. I think it happened to Truman Capote, who used to write mostly fiction and who now writes mostly fact. Capote's latest book, *In Cold Blood*, a detailed retelling of a grisly Kansas murder and of what happened to the two men who did it, is high-style reportage of the highest order—and I wish Capote had been willing to let things go at that. But for reasons not immediately clear, Capote announced, when his new book was published, that this time he had not merely written a book; he had invented a new art form. *In Cold Blood*, he said, was the world's first "nonfiction novel." Nor did he make this statement modestly. Word of the new art form, of Capote's six years of labor on the literary rock pile, of twelve arduous years of training his memory on Sears Roebuck catalogs until he no longer needed to take any notes, of the meticulous interviewing, the Herculean checking and re-checking of minute details, of the refulgent $2 million payoff

February 1966

of these labors, even of the incipient Pulitzer prize, seemed to appear almost simultaneously in every publication in America. I encountered twelve articles on Capote in national magazines in two weeks. What was most annoying about this massive huckstering bacchanal was that Capote himself appeared to be leading the grape stomp. Given the general mess of imprecision into which fiction and nonfiction have lately fallen, I suppose the invention of the "nonfiction novel" by somebody was probably inevitable. Unlabeled but very much with us for some time have been such spurious hybrids as the factual non-novel (*The Wall*); the fictional non-novel (*The Three Sirens*); the nonfictional non-novel (Robbe-Grillet and Burroughs) and fictional nonfiction (*Tony's Room*). We have even have had best sellers like *Games People Play*, a nonfictional, nonfactual non-novel, which I am not at all surprised to read will be made into a Broadway musical. Having over the years accepted all the rest of this stuff as some sort of fiction, one cannot start bullying poor Capote at this late date.

Still, I wish some other writer and not Capote had become the Cassius Clay of belles lettres. Elsewhere in life, immodesty no longer bothers me much. But in the case of a favorite author, I find myself becoming primly maiden-auntish. The next day two more Capote cover stories arrived in the mail. Why didn't, wouldn't, couldn't Capote for heaven's sake just shut up? I finally decided to go see him and find out.

Though I am not sure that I found out the entire answer—it is hardly a question one can ask a favorite author outright—I did learn part of it, and I have also played a new game and spent a beguiling afternoon with a man of unflagging charm. We toured Capote's luxurious new apartment, ate an excellent lunch, and visited several antique shops. In one of these the author bought himself a desk lamp that cost $5,500. The game was to try to remember every single thing that happened all afternoon without taking any notes.

As Capote says, note-taking during an interview impedes conversation. Long experience has taught me that it also leads to the buttered sleeve, the graphite pocket, and the uncrackable code. I decided to call on Capote without pad and pencil and then rush to the typewriter and see how much I could recall. I found I could remember literally everything—the full name of Capote's maid, for example, or the exact taste of the delicious steamed cucumbers in butter we ate for lunch—but that it didn't make a bit of difference. Of itself, total recall is of use to no writer except perhaps a court stenographer.

The quote I remember most vividly today out of all our ambling marathon chat is Capote's description of what it was like to have to watch two friends hanged. In five years of intensive interviews with his two murderers, they had become the two people he knew most intimately in all the world. "Going back to Kansas to watch the execution was unquestionably the most intense emotional experience of my life," he said. "But the boys wanted me there, so of course I had no choice. I spent the entire two days before the execution throwing up in my motel room. Telegrams kept arriving from the prison saying, 'Where are you?' And I couldn't move. But somehow when the time came, I got myself together and went there and spoke to them quite rationally, I think, and at the hanging I stood as close to them as I am to you now. When it was over, I started to cry and I couldn't stop. It was convulsive, like hiccups. They finally had to call a doctor to the prison to give me something and get me onto the plane home. And I had to fly all the way back to New York holding a pillow over my face because, you know, the tears just kept coming out. And yet, for the entire three days that I was throwing up and crying and carrying on, in another part of my mind I was sitting and quite coolly writing the story."

This description of the peculiar split between thinking and feeling that to some extent afflicts every journalist was one of the most honest confessions I'd ever heard a writer make.

A little later he made another. "About that nonfiction novel business, I wish I'd never said it. People didn't understand. But one has to do something." As he talked on about what it was that he, as a writer, had been trying to do with *In Cold Blood,* the peculiarly awful strain of the past six years became clear. Choosing to keep himself and his own feelings completely out of the book required total emotional isolation. In effect, the author had sentenced himself to emotional exile from the very people and place he was coming more and more to care most about. After six years of self-imposed exile in the third person, the need to shout "I, I, I" is understandable.

Since that afternoon I have thought a lot about Capote, about the nonfiction novel and especially about that $5,500 lamp. It is of Tiffany glass, a large, melted doily-shape of lavender and white wisteria blossoms drooping down over a bronze stalk. In every way a remarkable object of *virtu,* and as such I think it belongs to the right man. Virtuosity is Capote's main characteristic, and the distinguishing mark of his book as well. *In Cold Blood* is journalism arranged in the pattern of a novel, less a new art form than a new, delectable form of reportage enabling readers with tastes like mine both to have their cake and eat it. As for Capote's own tastes, when I imagine him now, sitting in the rich glow of his newest $5,500 treasure, I consider he has found the perfect object to write nonfiction novels by.

Hair Is Terribly Personal

❦

IN midtown Manhattan when I was growing up, a carnival-style pitchman used to hawk hair products on the sidewalk. His shill, a lady with remarkably long hair, sat silently on a low stool, her back to the crowd, the tips of her chestnut locks nearly brushing the pavement, while the pitchman assured his audience that this entire magnificent growth was due to the wonders of lanolin, pure wool fat, the greatest grease going for the human scalp. He clinched his beauty spiel by shouting hoarsely, "Next time ya happen to be in proximity to a sheep, run ya fingahs lightly tru da wool!" whereupon men and women would press forward from all sides happily waving dollar bills.

This was my first lesson that hair sells. The sight and subject of hair is in itself exciting. No matter how crudely you sell it, or what nonsense you have to say about it, what prices you charge or what indignities you inflict, you will have no trouble getting people's attention, including mine.

Hair is sexy. Hair brings one's self-image into focus; it is vanity's proving ground. Today boys grow long hair and get in fights with school principals. Girls press their hair on ironing boards and polish it on the beach. Women wear wigs. Bald men shave their heads. Some men wear bangs.

Hair is terribly personal, a tangle of mysterious prejudices. I hate men in bangs. I like men in long hair, crew cuts, thinning

October 1966

hair, and no hair. I can't stand long strands plastered over a bald pate. My daughter cried when she first saw Santa Claus. It turned out she was scared of beards. She still is. I like bushy beards, but not barbered ones. I'm scared of blue hair. I think mustaches are OK; sideburns awful. Why? What does it all mean? The other evening I met a distinguished psychiatrist and asked his opinion. "Well, I'll tell you," he said. "What I can't stand is the back of a woman's neck."

Hair sells today as never before. Hair products and hair-dressing for both sexes are booming. The vogue for fake Dynel hair, for wigs, wiglets, postiches, falls, switches, twists, and all other varieties of pin-on human hair is overwhelming and worldwide.

"It staggers me," says Mr. Kenneth, contemplating from the depths of his paisley salon the numbers of $400 and $500 hair-pieces he has sold. But for once the famed hairdresser has understated the case. Recently it was predicted that this year 30 million hairpieces will be sold in the United States alone, which suggests that more false hair may soon be pinned onto fashionable heads than is growing out of unfashionable ones.

The wholesale hair business is in a delirious uproar. I discovered this soon after contributing to the panic—both the wig industry's and my own—by acquiring one semihandmade fall of genuine human hair from a Mr. John wig boutique, one of hundreds of department store hair counters that have sprung up in response to the big hair boom.

A few days later I visited Manhattan's wholesale wig and toupee district and sat in a room containing over a million dollars' worth of human hair. My host, a professional hair buyer, described the place as "the Fort Knox of hair." I emerged from Fort Knox covered with lint and staggered myself by the enormity of it all. Several storerooms were piled to the ceiling with shoe boxes full of human hair. The hair came in many lengths and every shade from black through chestnut and red to platinum blond. It had all been collected from the heads of Korean peasant women, now the major suppliers of hair to the booming international market. There is not much European hair left. Oriental hair is considered technically superior in both body and luster to European hair; at least around Fort Knox it is. Thanks to a semisecret process invented four or five years ago, Oriental hair can now be bleached and dyed to match any color on the charts.

Indian and Indonesian hair are good too. The poorest-quality hair is Japanese. Red Chinese hair, which was officially embargoed by the United States last spring, used to appear on the market under the euphemism "European-made." Perhaps some of it still does. The hair business today is somewhat like the liquor business during Prohibition. There have been hair hijacks, hair heists, and even hairnappings. Legions of light-fingered Korean pickpockets have now taken to riding the buses armed with sharp scissors. And rumor has it that the custom requiring all Korean schoolchildren to have haircuts before beginning high school is also a reflection of the world-wide hair shortage.

Korean peasants will not sell their hair during spring and summer; they are too busy then, growing rice. But once the rice harvest is in, the hair harvest begins. Korean collectors then roam the countryside bargaining with farmers for hair to bring to the big international market in Seoul. It takes three years to grow an eighteen-inch crop of hair. Even people so poor they must sell their hair for money are not without vanity. Peasant women cut the hair from the center of the crown, where it won't show, then bind the long outside strands around the bald spot.

Ironically, much Korean and Indonesian hair, after being processed and made into curls, twists, falls, and so on, winds up back in Oriental department stores. Japanese women today are buying as many wigs and wiglets as American women do. When I asked the hair buyer why, he replied, "They want to look Italian!"

When a luxury liner was shipwrecked recently, newspapers described a woman running along the deck carrying nothing but a life preserver and her wig box. A woman used to be ashamed to wear a wig. Now it is a status symbol. Fashion models own four or five hairpieces, and jet-set types often have several dozen. Today's little girls are the first generation to whom false hair will seem as natural a bathroom artifact as a toothbrush. Unless, like my friend, you are happily set up in the wig business and sitting on top of a hoard of hair, it may be frightening to contemplate that next year 30 million more hairpieces will be sold, and 30 million the year after that.

Will all this put the hairdressers out of business? Nonsense. Nothing will put hairdressers out of business. The hairdressing business has just been enriched by 30 million tangled hairpieces. My own new hairpiece is at my hairdresser's right now, while I sit here with a rag around my head trying to figure out a way to beat the hair game.

A Funny-Ugh Movie

❦

NOBODY, including Freud, has ever fully explained laughter—thank God—but until recently one could be pretty sure of the meaning of "funny." If in doubt, one could always inquire, "Do you mean funny-peculiar, or funny–ha-ha?" Things are no longer that simple, and today we have a wildly fashionable category of humor that I would call funny-ugh. Sick jokes and novels about comedy rapists fall into the new category, and so, too, do most of the laughs in the current movie *The Loved One*. The hero keeps his lunch in an icebox full of dead dogs. A lovelorn embalmer Scotch-tapes notes on corpses. There is a bacchanal in a casket room, and later the cemetery director assaults the heroine while the organ booms love music and nude statues come to life and writhe concupiscently. The movie is a sort of mad Marx Brothers adventure in necrophilia, which is not at all to say that it does not also contain some giant yocks and savage stabs at the mortuary industry. My favorite scene is the cemetery board of directors' meeting at which Jonathan Winters, as the sanctimonious Blessed Reverend of Whispering Glades, announces grimly that, since all the consecrated ground will soon be filled up with loved ones, a more profitable new use for the real estate must be found. He therefore proposes building a senior citizens' village, pointing out that such a venture would insure a "brisk turnover." But wouldn't the new construction involve—ahem—"disinter-

October 1965

ment"? a board member inquires delicately, whereupon Winters leaps to his feet and shouts hoarsely, "Gentlemen, there's *got* to be a way to get those stiffs off my property!" By the end of the movie the way has been found: A dead astronaut is dug out of Whispering Glades so that, with all the blessings of Air Force recruitment, he can be rocket-launched into an "orbit of eternal grace" as Winters piously intones, "Resurrection *now!*"

In short, *The Loved One* is a funny-ugh movie about death. Aware that they may encounter some difficulty getting their money back, the movie producers have been running a series of test previews such as the one I attended last week, and they have chosen the ballyhoo line, "The motion picture with something to offend everyone." Although I am perfectly aware that such a slogan is designed merely to sell tickets, I take it as a personal challenge, nonetheless. Well, heh heh, I'm broadminded, and I agree that many of our funeral customs are ridiculous, so they're certainly not going to offend me! But they did. The picture left me feeling queasy, and for a time I couldn't figure out why. I rather enjoy gallows humor, and I am not offended by mortuary in jokes. Nor am I the least bit shocked by making fun of astronauts, who can take care of themselves. Perhaps, I thought, the answer (like so many other things) lies in that astonishing Disneyland of the dead (Jack Paar's name for Forest Lawn) on which Evelyn Waugh based his original satiric novel.

I telephoned the famous cemetery the next day and asked the public relations man about their official position on *The Loved One*. "We thought the book was sort of a quisling thing," he said. "But, alas, we haven't yet seen the picture." Since I was planning to see the movie again myself, it struck me that it would be fun to smuggle a couple of genuine Forest Lawn men into the next preview. "Don't wear black," I said, "or somebody at the studio might catch on."

"Don't worry," he replied cheerily. "We never do."

At the screening the Forest Lawn men seemed to enjoy

themselves, and as a result I had a better time myself. Indeed we all howled so merrily at characters like Liberace as an unctuous casket salesman ("Now, I can give you our eternal flame in either standard-eternal or perpetual-eternal") that it occurred to me that the ideal place to show *The Loved One* would be at a cemetery employees' company picnic. Any cemetery, it needn't be Forest Lawn. Fancy undertaking is big business in southern California, and I imagine the movie would be equally appreciated at the San Diego cemetery whose radio commercials plug the "choice-view sites," or at the Los Angeles establishment that puts up giant purple billboards bearing the single word: Foreverness.

But it turned out that the Forest Lawn men didn't like the movie any better than I did. "Frankly," they told me when it finally ended, "we think the picture could have been a lot funnier."

A distinguished art historian in our audience said he thought the movie was funny, all right, but not so funny as Forest Lawn. Ultimately I decided they were both right. The humor, the horror, and the vulgarity of cemeteries all depend a lot on what one is doing there. I have visited Forest Lawn, for example, both as a tourist and as a mourner. As a tourist, I agreed with Jack Paar. I hooted at the fake art and the awful sentimentality, and deplored the crass commercialism of selling plots in advance, a practice they call "pre-need counseling" but which sounds to me more like "pay now, die later." Yet I have come to Forest Lawn too in deepest grief, and at those times I found all the arrangements dignified and suitable in every particular. On the whole, I think cemeteries should put the needs and rights of mourners above the aesthetic sensibilities of casual tourists, and most of them do.

Of course, cemeteries do get a third class of visitor, and if one's prospect there is neither of touring nor of grieving but of moldering, I think one is obliged to be exceedingly modest in asserting rights or making demands of any kind. Beyond the right to will one's body to science, I'm not sure the dead have many funerary rights. The urge to supervise one's own disposal, however elegantly or forcefully or even touchingly it is expressed, is tinged with the same arrogance that afflicted the Pharaohs of Egypt.

One does not really own one's own death. It belongs to the living. It is their need to express their grief that must be contended with. Thus I think the only funeral custom I really object to—including insarcophagusment, orbits of eternal grace, and any other outrageous idea that cynical moviemakers or equally cynical funeral directors might dream up—is the denial of death, or rather the denial of the deep human need to mourn. The true queasy-making vulgarity of *The Loved One*, I think, lies in the fact that it mixes up jokes about our attitudes toward death, which are often absurd, with death itself, which never is. The Forest Lawn man had said proudly, "You get so caught up in the beauty of the place, you really forget you are in a cemetery." But when I go there, I don't want to forget. I want with all my heart to remember.

"Little Shirley Temple" Lives

🌷

"LITTLE Shirley Temple is not running," said Mrs. Shirley Temple Black on the morning that she announced she was going to run for Congress. She also made public her position on the war in Vietnam and on race riots, high taxes, drug-taking, LBJ, and pornography—she is against them.

Having talked to her recently myself, I am absolutely convinced she is against what she says she is against. Not only do I not question her sincerity, which is as convincing at thirty-nine as it was at five; often I heartily agree with her: There *should* be more women in Congress. But whether it is indeed Mrs. Black who is running, or whether it remains "little Shirley Temple" despite all the disclaimers, is, I am afraid, not up to the candidate to say.

Control of "little Shirley Temple" passed out of Mrs. Black's hands a quarter-century ago. The moppet belongs to the ages. The fact that Mrs. Black survives in northern California is merely an accident of history, a fortunate accident so far as conservative politics goes. Because of it, what would ordinarily be a minor contest in traditionally Republican San Mateo County is being watched with the most meticulous attention by political bosses of both parties all across America.

What attracts them is the spectacle of genuine myth-on-the-hoof, real living legend, or perhaps living fossil, a golden-curled pterodactyl left over from another era. "Little Shirley

November 1967

Temple" is the single most schmaltzy sweetmeat that the dream factory called Hollywood ever turned out. To create her, the mythmakers took the sentimental convention that a little child shall lead them and pumped it up, jazzed it up, and drove it home in the special way that only the movies can— with a stake through the heart.

President Roosevelt, who knew a potent image when he saw one, credited "little Shirley Temple" with helping to lift America out of the Great Depression of the 1930s. And yet the archetype of this vintage American myth is alive today, not living in Argentina but running for Congress in California.

All this is a weighty burden of legend and expectation to bear, even for someone who has been a working pro since age three. In gross tonnage, Shirley's "image" is roughly comparable to that of the Statue of Liberty. So it must be said at once that Mrs. Black bears it, hefts it, and fields it with charm, spirit, vivacity, good humor, health, and total unflappability— all characteristics that should be most helpful anywhere in Washington. "Anywhere," because one does not necessarily expect Mrs. Black's ambition to rest in the House of Representatives. Actors, even retired ones, head for stage center by instinct. The spotlight is their tropism. Edging, even shoving, toward it is "doing their thing." Look at Ronald Reagan.

In the 1930s, Hollywood history records, whenever a Shirley Temple movie was in front of the camera, Shirley's tireless mother always stood behind it, exhorting her tiny moppet to "sparkle, Shirley, sparkle!" I remembered this last week when I visited Mrs. Black at her home in suburban San Mateo County, deepest country-club country, an area that has been called a hotbed of social rest. The candidate received me in the spacious pool house of her home, and for the next two hours she scintillated steadily. The trouble with promising antipoverty funds to prevent future race riots, she said, is that it is like offering candy to a child who is having a tantrum. "The tantrum will stop, but the child, seeing he got by with it, determines to have another." Sparkle. "I'm neither a hawk nor a dove; I'm an owl." Sparkle. "I feel if I am elected to Congress, I cannot do much about this war, but I can do something to prevent the next Vietnam developing." Sparkle. "The President should listen more to his military experts. Only a small percent of our possible targets in North Vietnam have been bombed. Why haven't we mined the harbor at Haiphong?" Flash. Boom.

I preferred hearing Shirley recall the old movie-star days when the unreality of her life was *real*, when the studio took such enormous pains to protect the innocence of its five-year-old gold mine that one goddamn on the set meant instantaneous dismissal. "I'd hear Lionel Barrymore start in—he was in great pain, you know—and I'd think, great! I'm going home early again today." Sparkle. Between takes, Shirley was strictly confined to a sort of dollhouse-bungalow, which the studio had outfitted with pet rabbits, swings, sandpile. "So there I used to sit all day, playing with my rabbits, digging in my sandpile. I think now, if only I'd dug deeper, there was oil under that bungalow!"

If "little Shirley Temple" isn't running, neither is she dead. She has become part of the common subliminal experience of Americans of middle voting age, knotted tight into our national collective unconscious, curls bouncing, twinkle toes tapping, and in there to stay. Whether her presence there can get Mrs. Black into Congress is the interesting question to be decided in the special election this fall. Two of the ten candidates running against her have been desperate enough to go all the way to Vietnam to attract, or rather to distract, voters' attention. But it's no go. One of these unfortunates told me he was in a muddy Marine outpost near the DMZ and opened a copy of *Stars and Stripes* only to find a picture of Shirley Temple Black pouring coffee in Redwood City. What's a candidate to do?

In the final weeks of Mrs. Black's campaign, she has made her unflappable way through dozens of well-mown-lawn parties and *Kaffeeklatsches* in her richly populated (222,000 voters) district, talking optimistically and without letup of hawks, doves, owls, eagles, and all the other contemporary political fowl. The relentless twinkling makes me wonder if the candidate glows in the dark.

If "little Shirley Temple is not running," in a way her mother is. The child star, now grown up, has metamorphosed into the movie mother. It is she who now cries, "Sparkle, Shirley, sparkle!" to the blinking, blinkered, mired, confused, apathetic, complacent, frightened, uncertain, rootless American electorate. If I am right and this is so, the important question to ask about congressional candidate Shirley Temple Black is not "Is she for real?" but, "Are we?"

6

Why Can't Things Be Like They Never Were?

Sugar Tongs and the Gush of Steam

❧

IF you really want to have some fun—the surprising, sentimental kind—take a five-year-old on her first train ride. But don't make it Los Angeles (where I live) to San Francisco (a nice place to go, but too short and, alas, now too decrepit a ride). Make it right across the whole huge beautiful damn country, one edge to the other. Be sure, though, that you've done it all many times before in your childhood with your parents and that the reason you're doing it now with your own child, instead of getting on an airplane, is because you want her to taste this vanishing scene, and you want to taste it again, too.

Much of it hasn't changed at all. The tickets don't unroll in varicolored streamers from shoulder to knee anymore, and gone too are the little porthole windows in the upper berths, which is how I first looked out at America. But just about everything else is the same—the soft chimes for dinner, the musty plush, the triangular-folded towels, the little ladders with carpeted rungs that get you up into your upper berth, and the canvas lattice that keeps you there as you rocket and bump fitfully through the long, snug night.

Even the personnel is the same. Fred, our porter this time, looks like Krishna Menon and has been with the railroad forty-

December 1966

one years. He used to earn $37.50 a month, and after ten years as a Pullman porter, he got free uniforms. But Fred feels that in many ways it has been a good life. He has traveled, he is not a country boy any longer; all those miles are broadening, he has seen something of the world. Thanks to a lifetime on the trains, Fred says he can walk with assurance into any city in the world. For somewhat similar reasons, I feel the same way.

In the chilly twilight of our second day, climbing the beautiful, high, still, lonely mountains of northern New Mexico, our elderly conductor stopped by to bring some small presents for my daughter. Railroads have always been specially geared to children. They invented the family fare and the children's menu. They also provided my own first delighted encounter with archaic items like silver lump-sugar tongs and finger bowls, which I am happy to report still turn up automatically after every meal.

Handing over his packet of crayons and coloring books, our conductor made a fine Freudian slip, if such a term can be applied to so benign an old man. "There just ain't no railroad takes care of its patients—er, passengers—like the Santa Fe does," he told us.

There is much to be said for the feeling of being "taken care of" these days. And for that warm sense of being snugly encapsulated, happily cocooned, and out of time, you can't beat a long train ride. For people of my age, it is like being towed cross-country in a security blanket, and the feeling helps make up for the two days and three long nights in which the child sleeps peacefully in the upper berth while you toss and turn in the lower, wondering whether it is their old roadbed or your old bones that are really keeping you awake.

It was not always going across country with a father and mother. It was going off to summer camp, in sleeping cars with names like Fort Ticonderoga and Lake Winnipesaukee, dangling that new toy, the Yo-Yo, down through the thick brown curtains of the upper berth after lights out. Then going off to college, folding the first fur-trimmed coat with the lining-side out and placing it tenderly on the overhead racks, then sinking fat and terrified, nibbling on a forbidden chocolate bar, into the seat of scratchy green plush. It was sneaking off with my roommate to the Atlantic City YMCA to say good-bye to a soldier during the war. It was riding with a young husband from New York to Chicago to meet relatives neither of us had ever seen.

That happened on the Twentieth Century Limited, a great old train that doesn't even exist in its old form anymore. When we got into Chicago this time, we transferred to the Pennsylvania Limited, and we arrived not in Grand Central but in beautiful Pennsylvania Station, which doesn't exist in its old form anymore, either.

The Super Chief is almost the last of the deluxe passenger trains. The old place names on the timetable—Albuquerque (will the feathered Indians still be out on the drowsy platform selling moccasins?); the long tunnel over the top of Raton Pass; the beautiful steel bridge at Fort Madison, Iowa, where we cross the Mississippi (the Indians were gone, but the broad river was still full of migrating waterfowl)—all intensified my feelings of nostalgia. It feels as if you are rumbling across America and rumbling backward, too, in time, making your rocking way down long, overheated corridors, pushing open the heavy doors, feeling the rush of cold air and grit, hearing the gush of steam and the train whistles in the night and the clickety-clack, echoing back, echoing back, as you drift off to sleep at last in cool fresh sheets and pink-brown blankets of indescribable hue.

The trip backward in time had begun even before we got aboard. Making ticket reservations (to Chicago, by telegraph, and presumably in dot-and-dash Morse code) we were already talking again in the archaic vocabulary of "space," as in drawing room, and "pieces," as in luggage. My daughter and I had five pieces, and we drove them from home to a Los Angeles freeway exit I had never even used before.

There was empty old Union Station standing just as I

remembered it but hadn't seen it for over twenty years. The Rip Van Winkle feelings deepened. Though there weren't really any steamer trunks or lap robes or beribboned hatboxes among the five pieces that Fred stowed expertly in our small, softly lighted, stainless-steel and khaki-enamel and pink-brown space, the nostalgia was so powerful that the train began to seem even older than it actually was. I would not have been overly surprised had we ended our journey at night in a howling blizzard, then to be wrapped in great furs and whisked off by sled toward the lights twinkling in the snowy distance.

Eating delicious mountain trout and drinking coffee at our first railroad dinner, I realized how very many of the things I like I had first experienced on the trains; not only trout and finger bowls and sugar tongs, but Lake Superior whitefish and ice-cream bricks; thick china and heavy napery; stainless-steel sinks and well-lit mirrors and even the exact shade of cream-khaki-bronze wall enamel that I tried in vain to duplicate in flat paint through fifteen years of marriage. In a sense, I have been on the railroad all my life, like Fred. For me, too, though I don't know why, the train is a moving metaphor of life itself.

The original idea of the trip, as I said, was to take my daughter on her first train ride. But by the time the journey ended, I realized that the five-year-old we were really entertaining was not Kathy but me.

In theory, it is a good idea to let everyone's five-year-old me out for some fun occasionally, but in practice it hardly ever happens. In fact, one of the nicest things about our train trip was the discovery that my own five-year-old me was still in there after all these years.

The Nearest Faraway Place

❦

Smog-sick and dizzy from the blink of neon, unsteady and wanting time out in America, midsummer 1967, I have come again to Ireland. It is my fourth visit in five years. I am drawn to this island like a cart to a horse. It is not that I am myself Irish. Neither grandmother nor tradition tugs at me. It is because I am American that I am drawn here. In Ireland I seem to find something of lost America.

This is the way it used to be, I think to myself, awakening under heavy sheets of cool linen, hearing the clop-clop of horses on cobbles, spreading pots of thick butter on brown bread. This is the way it used to be, the low, courteous voices. "Hello. Good morning. Did you sleep well? Yes, certainly, we will. We will indeed." In America we have amputated these courtesies from trivial chat. A pity.

This morning on the Galway Road our car is halted by the flagman of a repair gang. A caravan of tinkers is camped alongside, their raggle-taggle washing spread out on a thornbush. Watching them loll about and drowse and pick flowers, I think how far off, and by contrast how feeble, America's flower children and their cult of flower power seem. Black power is far away too. And so is the unbearable struggle of hawk against dove.

When the flagman waves us on, he looks into each car and he smiles. That personal smile unsnarls for me a thousand miles

September 1967

of freeway tension. All sorts of things unknot for an American in Ireland. Time unspools. Nerves unwind. The rictus relaxes. Jaws unclench. I know that Irishry itself is a knotted bolus of tension and contradiction, treachery, accusation, drink, brag, and the pursuit of dreams. I know that simple joys do not imply a simple place and that Ireland is the citadel of paradox in Europe. We were speaking one morning of De Valera when an Irish senator said fiercely, "The only time Dev ever tells the truth is when he contradicts himself." Would Fulbright put it that way about Johnson?

No, Ireland is not at all a simple place, and in many ways it is spare and sad. It has no wealth, no power, no stability, no influence, no fashion, no size. Its only real arts are song and drama and poem. But Limerick alone has two thousand ruined castles and surely that many practicing poets.

"Really why Ireland has no pictures is that it has no walls," one of them told me. "It is purely a verbal culture." But the vein of literary tradition is the deepest and richest in Europe, begun in the ancient bardic schools. This oral tradition endured through all the centuries of war, it lived even through the great famines when all else died, it produced some of the greatest poets and, since Shakespeare, all the greatest playwrights in English, it infused an entire nation with a passion for words.

Enter any pub and the language rivets. "Don't provoke me," I heard one man warn, "or they'll have to dig me out of you."

One day, walking in Cork, a friend claimed you could enter any Irish pub, say absolutely anything, and be sure of an interesting reply. The phrase we agreed on was: "I was thinking yesterday of the King of Siam. . . ." We turned into the next pub and tried it. "I was thinking yesterday of the King of Siam. . . ."

"Ah, dreaming of Thigh Land, were you," said a man standing at the bar.

Ireland has great richness, too, of time, of natural human

(154

courtesy and dignity and of unspoiled natural beauty. It is a country rich exactly where we are poor. It is the obverse of America, our flip side. Change all our darks to lights, make a montage of all our negatives, imagine the precise positive to that negative, and you will have an image of Ireland.

The newspaper arrives. Fulbright has called us a sick society. I hope he is wrong, but for the moment it is enough that I am away. The fluid light shifts on a wet-cold landscape of flocks and hills. Haycocks pin down the glimmering aftergrass. A boy by the roadside offers a string of wild mushrooms threaded on a green weed, and we eat them raw—the cleanest taste in the world. *New York stews in killer smog*, the newspaper says.

Again the light changes. The skies wheel with flights of rooks and crows. A group back home has proclaimed send-a-rat-to-Congress week. Now the clouds above have arranged themselves into a mackerel sky. In Ireland the light has legs. Isn't this the way it used to be in America before the spoilers took hold? Isn't this the way it used to be in the romantic past before the polluted present, before the lakes became cesspools, the rivers sewers, and the skies a roof of noxious fumes?

And it happened so fast! As John Huston says, "It all got out of hand within one generation—my own lifetime."

Huston is Ireland's most vigorous American transplant. But Ireland blooms with truant Americans. One was a three-martini-lunch man in the Madison Avenue squirrel cage, he told me, until the day he half sobered up in an airport, staggered to the counter, and asked the clerk for "a ticket to the nearest faraway place." Fortunately it was the Boston airport, and Aer Lingus was not asleep at its post.

Ireland does not charm all men. To Actor Robert Morley, presently in Ireland filming *Sinful Davey*, the place is "Disneyland run by the Pope!" But Morley, of course, is English.

The commodity Ireland and America traffic in most heavily is nostalgia, and nostalgia is always strongest for the place one never was. I learned this final Gaelic paradox on my last day in

155)

Ireland when I traveled with a friend to revisit his boyhood home under the hills of Clare. Like so many of his countrymen, he has long been a voluntary exile. "People are raised here on fancies and dreams," he says. "Great for boyhood, but a man needs realities and hardness—so he leaves."

All around Clare the countryside glowed gold and green. Wood pigeons flapped out of a ruined castle. Thick yew-fingers poked up from an old graveyard, and as I clambered in the wet grass, a nettle stung my ankle. I rubbed it with a dock leaf, the remedy that mysteriously grows beside its own hurt, and later we climbed a hilltop to look out across the afternoon to Knock Na Fearna, the fairy mountain.

Pigeon, nettle, dock leaf, and castle—all of these were new to me. It was *his* landscape, *his* source and childhood we were seeing, not my own. I am a child of mid-Manhattan. Yet I felt suffused with the most intense, lump-in-throat nostalgia. As we drove away, I wondered, and then I was quite sure. I knew which of us found the castle the harder to leave. He, after all, had left it once before.

Triviality Has Never Seemed Less Trivial

🌷

Oh, today, for a bear on ice skates! A spinning ballerina drilling holes into the floor. A tenor shattering chandeliers, or a smiling tap dancer who barely moves, though a sound like a shower of pebbles shimmies from his shoes. If only Heinz Arntz, the marathon pianist who is pushed, playing, around the world, would come tinkling into town. If only the Nerveless Nocks would loom down from their great sway poles, balancing their trayloads of pink sugar syrup, or if I could see ageless Satchel Paige creak once more and let fly his wonderful "disappearing ball."

Triviality has never seemed less trivial than it does this spring, nor innocent nonsense more alluring.

It is circus time again, and more than ever I find myself longing to see all sorts of sideshow marvels, bygone acts, and flyblown vaudevilles. The silly acts, like the symphony orchestra that spouts water from a tuba and emits a flight of sparrows from the bull fiddle. The precarious acts, like the Nocks, who do their acrobatics atop sixty-foot flexible masts, or like the juggler who dashes insanely back and forth across the stage spinning dozens of plates on dozens of whirling sticks. The violent acts, like the dwarf cowboy in chaps who, with a sudden maniacal lunge, sinks his teeth into the tall

March 1968

cowboy's shin. The scary acts, like the pickpocket who glides between the crowded nightclub tables and somehow lifts wallets, pens, jewels, even wristwatches without our feeling a thing. When he has whipped us all into a panic frenzy like frightened fish, he suddenly plunges a rubber dagger into his wrist and sprays us with fake blood.

There are some marvelous acts in which nothing at all happens—the "performing" dog who refuses to budge, the haughty magician whose tricks never work. In other marvelous acts, everything happens. The illusionist of the Moscow Circus makes fourteen women, a live lion, and a one-horse shay materialize in midair.

There is true circus surrealism in the man who pulls mandolins and bananas out of his coat, in Mr. Electric, whose fingers and mouth and ears make light bulbs light, or in the horde of white mice who are loaded aboard a small airplane. The craft circles the tent a few times before its motor sputters and dies dealing us a true heart-thumping moment until all the mice come gently floating down in little parachutes.

Thinking of these things, and why I want so much to see them this particular spring, my mind suddenly snaps back to another spring long ago, when a boy and a girl used to slip away from school and sneak uptown to Yankee Stadium. We were eleven years old, and our single blissful objective was to watch Joe DiMaggio bat. Galileo staring at the moons around Jupiter could not have focused with more passionate intensity than did the boy and I on various sections of Joe. We devoted an entire afternoon to his wrists. We reserved another whole day for his feet. We split a doubleheader between knees and elbows. We inspected Joe's elbow the way the poet once gazed at his mistress's eyebrow. Today I understand that most of the joy of those long, thrilling, sun-slanted afternoons came not from watching Joe, but from our relief at not having to face what we couldn't bear to look at—each other. What we really sought so desperately was distraction.

Seeking it again today, I wish I still had the tunnel vision of an eleven-year-old. I wish I could still find the same blinkered delight in watching one man, or one bear, do one single simpleminded trick.

Alas, I have grown more discriminate. *Any* circus act will no longer do. Certain standard stunts have become definitely unappealing—the woman who catches bullets in her teeth; the fellow who chews up light bulbs and razor blades. Nor do I relish knife throwers, bullwhip artists who flay the cigarette inch by inch from the lady's smiling lips, child contortionists or wrestlers-in-mud. These things lack the essential innocence of the nonstop pianist or the ice-skating bear.

Well then, I wonder, would a wire walker still be fun to watch? How about a fire walker or a ropedancer? A stunter in an air circus would not, I think, be spring tonic for me today. Neither would the illusionist who sets a woman on fire.

Drilled dressage horses are no longer wholly satisfactory either. They do something that is too unnatural: They have been too much forced into their impossible grace, like the bound foot of the Chinese bride. The impossible may be made possible by a miracle, by a trick, or by superhuman skill. But not by the might of man.

Seals and tigers dressed up like men in hats and coats look only humiliated in the association. Elephants ought not to be doing tricks at all. They are the aristocracy of the jungle. An elephant on his hind legs mocks both animals and man.

Back in the spring of 1938, even before I was focusing so hard on Di Maggio's elbow, Satchel Paige had an arm worth $150,000 to the major leagues. Very possibly Satch is the greatest pitcher who ever lived. But because his arm was the wrong color, Satch was condemned to be a lifetime circus act. His uniform just said "Satchel" and he was advertised as "guaranteed to strike out the first nine men." If he didn't, he didn't get paid.

This spring, as always—it is his forty-second season in baseball—Satch is preparing to put his own circus on the road again. He likely does not throw the disappearing ball any more, the one that goes so fast it just burns up, like a meteor. But I feel like going to see him anyhow, just in case. The need to see Satch or the spinning ballerina or the bear is a desperate lunge out of reality, an attempt to see something other than what stares up at us this spring from every front page. I'm tired of looking death in the face and starving children in the eyes. If I goggle at parachuting mice or the disappearing ball, I may not see the bodies laid in rows by roadsides. If I listen to the nonstop piano, I may not hear the monstrous news reports of "victory" by "body count."

This is why this week I write about bears on ice. The real distraction I seek is distraction from being distraught.

An Ordeal to Choke a Sword-Swallower

🌺

ALTHOUGH I am otherwise reasonably healthy, there is something about Christmas that always makes me get sick. Last year it was a backache, the year before, an earache—my annual Wassail collapse is becoming a family tradition. This past Christmas I overreached myself and wound up not only sick in bed, but upside-down and miserable as well. My own description of my symptoms sounded to me like the label off a patent-medicine bottle. The main complaint was an off-and-on unexplained cough I've had for seven years, and the upshot of my talks with several doctors was to go to the hospital so that definitive tests could be made.

In case you missed the bronchoscopy and the bronchogram on *Dr. Kildare*, what it means is that first they slide a metal tube with a light on the end of it down into your windpipe in order to examine your lungs in living color. Later they get you to inhale a couple of lungfuls of thick, white, luminous goo that shows up in incredibly detailed X rays, which make your chest look like something that should be on display at Marineland.

The procedure is a hospital commonplace, but it can require a lot of fuss, and—should the patient turn out to have both a very powerful gag reflex and large front teeth (I could have told them if someone had bothered to ask)—it may also involve quite a crescendo of drugs. My own recollection, as clearly as I can remember it, is of an oratorio for massed barbiturates, and my brains felt scrambled for weeks afterward. It was an ordeal to befuddle a hophead and choke a sword-swallower, and though I do now know what was causing my cough (nothing too serious), I wasn't sure until this morning that I would ever fully get over the tests.

The patient is, of course, warned that the tests are going to make him feel bad. Part of the recommended post-hospital therapy is to spend as much time as possible lying on a slant board, feet fifteen inches higher than head. Although medicine calls this "postural drainage," Elizabeth Arden calls the same thing "the beauty angle," so I figured it couldn't be too unpleasant. I borrowed a board from a ladies' gym, set it in front of the TV set, clambered on, wrapped myself tightly in a blanket to ward off chilly floor-level drafts, hooked my wrapped feet under the ankle strap, and slowly let myself lie back. This posture is ideal for being fired into orbit or buried at sea, but it turns out to be useless for anything else, including reading, TV, or even light conversation. When one is lying at floor level and upside down on the dining room floor, the first thing that drains away is social aplomb. One becomes a sort of elongated hassock for children and dogs to trip over, and since one has, after all, "passed" the dreaded tests, there is not even much sympathy to be garnered from clucking friends. All in all, there has been plenty of time to think in the past few weeks, and my thoughts were surely stimulated by the rush of blood to the head. What I thought about chiefly was me and doctors.

It was a twenty-four-hour theme and I couldn't turn it off. At night I had grotesque dreams straight out of old-time vaudeville: terrified patient strapped onto operating table: "Doctor, I'm dubious." Doctor (leering): "Glad to meet you, Mr. Dubious." (Followed by loud clanking of fire irons, hacksaws, and other surgical gear.)

By day, when vertical, I hunted out medical stories in the newspapers. One I remember vividly was a front-page announcement of some research by a couple of distinguished social scientists who warned that TV shows like *Ben Casey* and *Dr. Kildare* were doing serious damage to the American doctor image. By portraying the physician not as kindly, wise, white-haired old Dr. Christian but as a human being who gets hungry and sleepy and even sometimes makes mistakes, TV was accused of helping to destroy the awe, the charisma, the "social distance" that is vital to the doctor-patient relationship. Though upside-down, I was still dubious. Certainly faith is important and itself therapeutic, but my faith is always stronger in the mortal man than in the high priest, however glittery his charisma or white his hair. Or at least that is the case when I am vertical. The difficulty with becoming a patient is that as soon as you get horizontal, part of your being yearns not for a mortal doctor but for a medicine man.

The real trouble with the doctor image in America is that it has been grayed by the image of the doctor-as-businessman, the doctor-as-bureaucrat, the doctor-as-medical-robot, and the doctor-as-terrified-victim-of-malpractice-suits. I have no suggestions as to what the medical profession as a whole can do about this; it may be a matter for each doctor to grapple with individually. The one doctor I know of who has materially improved his or her image is a lady pediatrician who got so mad at her office medical linen service (she had just been accused of the theft of 700 towels) that in fury she canceled the service and bought a black uniform. She decorated this with bright felt cutouts of hearts and flowers and sewed a big red lollipop up the back. She says her patients love her new image, and so do I.

I would not think of having a doctor I didn't like. The reason has nothing to do with his professional competence, which I cannot judge anyhow. My liking him won't make him a better doctor, but I think it will make me a better patient.

I don't require him to have a lollipop up his back, but I do want my doctor to listen very carefully to what I have to say; to tell me every bit he can about what he is looking for and what he finds, and when he doesn't know, say so.

One day last week, I got up off the board and found to my horror that I could hardly move my neck. I seemed to be wearing a high choke collar of painful swollen glands. My first thought was that all the poison had drained out of my lungs up into my neck. This odd new symptom, coming after all my other complaints, made me fear that the real trouble must be flaming hypochondria. But, I reminded myself, I like my doctor and, after all, I couldn't move my neck. It was last Friday by the time he had checked out this new complaint and called back to say he thought it probably was some sort of virus. The upside-down board had nothing to do with it. "Let me know Monday how you are," he said. "As for treatment, I have absolutely nothing to suggest."

My neck and I spent an uncomfortable but uneventful weekend together, and when I called my doctor today, his office was humming with a new crop of Monday morning patients, so I just left a message with the nurse: Mrs. Alexander feels fine.

7

Getting Around

The Roman Astonishment

❦

It was fitting that our flight to Rome put down at Lourdes; tourists bound for Rome need a miracle. How is the new-comer to deal with Rome? What is one to make of this marble rubble, this milk of wolves, this blood of Caesars, this sunrise of Renaissance, this baroquery of blown stone, this warm hive of Italians, this antipasto of civilization? Rome's riches are in too immediate juxtaposition. Under the lid of awful August heat, one moves dizzily from church to palace to fountain to ruin, a single fly at a banquet, not knowing where to light.

Dropped into the middle of so great a plural, one must find the singular. I found him on the third day, and when I found him, he led me to all the plurals. He showed me Rome.

We had driven up into the lovely Campidoglio, a piazza so perfect the Renaissance itself appears to hang suspended in high, peach-colored light. "Six centuries before Christ, here stood the greatest temple of the Roman world," intoned a guide. "This square was designed by Michelangelo. In the center, the bronze statue of Marcus Aurelius . . ."

The brazen sun clanged and reverberated off the bronze emperor. Then I turned and began to walk alone very slowly around the rim of the piazza, thinking of nothing except the cool of these colonnades. Suddenly, an unsuspected courtyard, splashing water. Within, a worn and bearded stone giant reclined above a shadowed pool. He was eighteen feet long, his

September 1967

repose overwhelming. I have never seen such profound weariness nor heavy grace. Water gushed from a lion's head black with moss. There were dolphins. A mother sat on the edge of the basin feeding her baby. A policeman removed his white kepi to dunk his head. A marble pope gazed down. But it was the mysterious, melancholy giant who was sovereign here.

Before I came back to visit him that afternoon I had found out who he was: Marforio, an ancient river god, possibly the oldest fountain in Rome. Marcus Aurelius himself knew him, and Virgil; perhaps all the Caesars. During the many sacks of Rome, he lay unmolested in the Forum, seeing all. In 1594 he was hauled up the hill, and later his courtyard was built around him.

When I returned to the Campidoglio after lunch, the courtyard was closed. Tourists moved over the piazza like drugged insects on a painted plate, and behind the heavy gates I could imagine Marforio drowsing, too, in his cage of sun-warm stone. But I made a vow to Marforio, to his sightless eye and passive hand. I would come back and see him every day I was in Rome. He would give focus and center to my random sightseeing.

On each visit I saw something more. How noble he was, and how soft his old stone. The city of Rome looks operatic, an endless sequence of stage sets waiting for the singers to appear. But Marforio is not operatic. He is classical, pagan, reposed. A pair of standing, curly-bearded satyrs bracket the river god and define his gentleness by their debauchery. Two piddling dolphins add size. The prim pope bestows freedom. The green moss muzzle of the lion sprouts ferns from each nostril for fantasy. The attendants who groom him hide their scrub brush under the mighty left hand. The river god's extended right foot has obviously been restored, but the other foot lies half-hidden beneath his robe, its broken toes stubbed off against the centuries.

By night the piazza blazes with operatic light, and inside his courtyard Marforio, too, is melodramatically "lit" for evening.

(168

This is not a success. Underwater spotlights ripple without mercy over the face and body of the god. In the hard glare he lies impassive, submitting—a blank-faced nude in a strip show. The lion, on the other hand, is loving it. Spread-eagled, his ferny nostrils underlit, he lifts the snout of a gargoyle come alive. The joy of the lion perfectly mocks the agony of the old god. He was made for sunlight, not for this. His false foot and nose show cruelly in this light, which is so theatrical, so strong, so insulting, so *Italian*. But he will endure this night. Time has already done to him all that time can.

"You know, of course, that these *gigantica* are not considered first-rate art," a Roman friend remarks. I say it is not the art but my own response that matters. In finding Marforio I have found astonishment. Marforio is making me see Rome. The fountains spout higher, the marble flesh grows warm, the fading frescoes glow again, and the winds of baroquery blow wilder at all the gesturing angels.

This is what holidays, travels, vacations are about. It is not really rest or even leisure we chase. We strain to renew our capacity for wonder, to shock ourselves into astonishment once again.

Then one morning I discovered the incomparably graceful Villa Giulia, where a great trove of Etruscan art is arrayed in the most beautiful museum space I know. Implement and ornament, beasts and striding warriors—the Etruscans had seen all and done it all before anybody! I wandered in a daze of wonder. The perfection of every single object was such that the faintest lapse—one slightly squat vase, for example, in a gallery of hundreds—brought me rushing up to its glass case.

On this day, I had intended to go back to the Campidoglio to see Marforio as usual, but abruptly I decided not to, to hurry on to other monuments instead. "He won't really mind," I thought. "He has been betrayed a thousand times before." The remainder of my Roman holiday became one sellout after another. I betrayed Marforio again in the Piazza Navona, sold him false at Castel Sant' Angelo, deceived him at

Saint Peter's among the Bernini colonnades, tricked him at the Vatican Museum, mocked him with Marcus Aurelius, was disloyal in the Piazza di Spagna, traitorous at the Temple of the Twelve Gods, false at the Pantheon, faithless at the Fontana di Trevi, and standing beneath the Caravaggios in the church of Santa Maria del Popolo, was instantly untrue once more.

The treachery of it! I marvel to myself now, back home, far from Rome, still not quite believing it all happened, still puttering in my guidebooks at summer's end. The great, noble, enduring Marforio, reduced onto a glossy souvenir postcard, lies here on my desk, and looking at it, I wonder if I will ever get back to him again. I think I will. If not, he will get over it long before I do.

Three Strangers in Selma

❧

NOBODY can fully anticipate Selma, Alabama. No matter how well you have monitored your TV, read your Bible, or steeled your heart, you are in for all kinds of surprises the moment you hit town. My first came in Sheriff Clark's office, where I went to pick up the press pass I knew I, as a white person, would need in order to get inside the Negro compound. I had expected police headquarters to look like an arsenal; instead it looked like an opera star's dressing room. The walls were papered with telegrams to the sheriff, about equally divided pro and con. What was surprising was that the scourges and hosannas were all posted with equal, impartial pride, as if Sheriff Clark saw himself primarily as some sort of monstrous diva.

My pass was number 258, and the deputy who issued it remarked slyly that 256 of the passes had gone to male reporters and politely warned me to "watch out for them white niggers, ma'am." He turned out to be wrong on both counts. There were several other women reporters, and in reality my pass turned out to be a ticket to sanctuary. Inside the Negro compound was the one place in Selma where I felt completely safe.

At the dividing line between the black and white sections of town, the singing Negroes stood pressed up against a line of wooden barricades. The opposing line of grim state troopers

March 1965

stood back a ways, leaving a no-man's-land in which the pack of photographers and reporters could freely roam. I didn't stay long. The troopers and the townspeople behind them looked menacing enough, but it was less fear than embarrassment that drove me away. I felt ashamed to be a spectator at this kind of confrontation, even though that was the reason I had come.

When I returned there very early the next morning, the day of the memorial service for the slain minister, the Reverend James Reeb, the massed might of Alabama law and order had magically vanished, leaving nothing behind but a vast mulch of squashed oranges, pop bottles, and paper cups. Far down the littered street the familiar line of Negroes stood where they had been for almost a week, still singing and swaying, many caped in raggedy blankets against the dawn chill. But without the barricades they didn't look so heroic now, merely forlorn. Nonviolence is less impressive without violence.

To help the Negroes in their march, hundreds of religious people had come from all over the country, and now they were making last-minute plans in a church basement at the far end of the street. I arrived just in time to see one minister whack another over the head with a rolled-up newspaper. As the victim doubled up on the floor, the circle of nuns and clerics leaned gravely forward. This was, of course, a demonstration of self-defense. I doubt if anyone in the room seriously feared an attack by troopers, even Alabama ones, but the sudden, unexplained disappearance of the police that morning may have reminded everyone how easy it had been a few days earlier for hoodlums to club another cleric to death without interference on a lighted downtown street. The ministers ended their meeting by singing "We Shall Overcome." In the dim-lit basement it sounded like a Gregorian chant.

We filed upstairs, and far up at the head of the street, behind the still-singing Negroes keeping vigil at the Line, we could see squad cars shimmering in the early morning sunlight. The mysterious reappearance of the troopers was no more ominous than their disappearance, and when the ministers began to form ranks, I impulsively took off my press pass and joined up.

Hand-holding would have been awkward since some marchers carried breviaries or prayer shawls, so we all linked arms and began walking forward, five abreast. We had three or four long blocks to reach the Line. As we walked, the man on my right introduced himself as a seminarian from Minnesota. The man on my left, a Negro, represented the Catholic Interracial Council of Chicago. We also had an Episcopalian and a nun. When she told the rabbi in front of her, "You're my protector, now," we all smiled. Everyone seemed quite relaxed, and I thought I was, too.

Without my realizing it, we had reached the barrier, and suddenly I locked eyes with a big, jowly trooper holding a billy club and wearing an orange hat. It hit me then for the first time that one of the arms I was holding belonged to a very tall, black, mustached Negro, and for a long moment my stomach was filled with butterflies, first of fear, then of shame at my fear. I looked away. When I did look back at Jowls, he dropped his eyes almost at once. I tried it with his neighbor, Shorty, then with Blue Eyes. The same thing happened. Quickly tiring of a game I've not played since third grade, I thanked my new friends for letting me march with them, stepped out of line, pinned my pass back on, turned back into a reporter, and began making notes.

That afternoon the ministers held their first memorial service for the Reverend James Reeb at the African Methodist Episcopal Church. Behind the pulpit sat an ecumenical rainbow: a monsignor, the chief Unitarian minister in the United States, the presiding bishop of the Episcopal Church, the robed primate of the Greek Orthodox Church, assorted Baptist and Methodist leaders, a rabbi from Canada, and, finally, Martin Luther King. Before the service we sang spirituals and civil rights songs. It was hot, the stained glass windows were open, and in each niche perched a priest clapping his hands and shouting out A-Amen in fundamentalist fervor. When the assorted eulogies and prayers and readings were finally over, the Methodist minister who was leading the service told us that the memorial would close by having the rabbi say a benediction, after which we would all join in singing "We Shall Overcome."

But in everyone's combined weariness and exultation, things got a bit mixed up. We were all on our feet, holding crossed-over hands, swaying and singing, before the rabbi could reach the pulpit. The surprises overwhelmed me as I watched the bearded primate intoning the moving Negro anthem; felt the two men on either side of me tugging my crossed arms; even heard my own voice seeming to soar. Then suddenly, as we were all softly humming the final verse, the rabbi got started. Over the throbbing, church-filling, ecumenical hum of more than four hundred nuns and clerics, we could clearly hear him intone the kaddish, the ancient Hebrew prayer for the dead.

When the incredible moment ended, I thought that maybe this was just what the Reverend James Reeb might have liked to hear. I fumbled for my notebook because I did not want ever to forget the names of the two strangers whose hands I'd held in Selma that day.

The Three-Hundred-Year Weekend

🌷

As one who really appreciates weekends, I had come to think the great ones all require the same basic props: seclusion, repose, a jug of wine, thou. But since we are old and good friends, I listened politely when the psychologist told me about the Marathon and promised that "it will be the greatest weekend of your life."

He explained that the Marathon, or "three-hundred-year weekend," is a new form of nonstop therapy in which a dozen or so strangers shut themselves up in a room with a couple of trained therapists and try to practice total honesty for thirty or forty hours at a stretch. Privacy, save in the bathroom, is nonexistent. Meals are eaten on laps; catnaps, if necessary, take place right on the floor; alcohol is forbidden. This unremitting intimacy is said to force out buried emotions that otherwise would take months of couch time to surface. Indeed, my friend claimed the psychic payoff of the Marathon was so immense it could scarcely be put into words. I said I could put it in one word—aauugghh—but he only smiled.

My friend is a good psychologist all right, I reflected a few days later, as I found myself climbing the front steps of his house at six o'clock one Saturday morning, wearing old clothes and carrying a pillow for catnaps. "Welcome to our space capsule," the doctor cried and introduced me to my fellow travelers—a minister, a garage attendant, an ex-movie actress, a computer wizard, several housewives, two or three businessmen, and two practicing psychiatrists, there to learn the new Marathon technique. We were old and young, black and white, singles and pairs—so diverse that we looked like a troupe of actors about to begin rehearsals for *Grand Hotel*. For the next thirty hours that room was our whole world.

We sat in a circle on chairs, pillows, and floor, freely changing positions according to instructions. As the lights of Hollywood blinked off-on-off outside our windows, we moved through a sort of long, slow-motion square dance, and each time our group repatterned in different chairs, we went deeper into ourselves, peeled off another layer or two of defensive reserve, and drew emotionally closer. This was a human pressure cooker, and by midafternoon the pot was really bubbling. Soon I felt tears, laughter, and rage spurting inside me with unaccountable force, as if subterranean veins of emotion were rupturing one by one. Although I swiftly lost track of time, peak emotional moments stand out: A pair of young lovers tried to describe their feelings and I was suddenly so moved, I almost wept. Another time I filled up with fury and was shocked to hear my own voice snap at a perfect stranger, "Liar! I don't like you because you have not been telling us the truth." Other people joined me; I became the lead hound of a baying pack: what's more I *liked* the feeling. Eventually we drove this man to truthful tears. He was contemplating a divorce, but he had been denying that he felt guilty about the effect it would have on his daughters. Finally he came clean, exhausted himself, felt better, and fell asleep on the floor like a weary child. Another time, listening to the squabbling of a long-married couple, I suddenly felt so nauseated I literally had to lie flat on the floor and hold on to keep from throwing up.

Our laughs were outsize too, and I remember one mad moment when a Negro man leapt to his feet and began struggling to express his feelings about the white people in the room. He was fully prepared for rejection, he said, by a lifetime of experience. Suddenly this black man whirled and bellowed, "What I can't stand is all your *acceptance!* I don't know what to *do!*" It was grotesque, absurd, a scene from Jean Genet.

My own responses were weird, too. I ate ravenously. Though I'd had only three hours' sleep the night before, I grew progressively more awake. Then suddenly, at about hour 20, I was overcome by a yawning fit, crawled under the piano with my pillow, and instantly slept. When I awoke only minutes later, the strange view of the underside of the piano was disturbingly familiar. Then I remembered that when I was a little girl, the cave underneath my composer father's piano in our living room had been my special hideaway. Simultaneously it struck me how eerily the Marathon was recapitulating my own life. The piano was my childhood lair; the girl in love was *me* in first love; the young bride was me as a bride, secretly writing "Mrs." in front of my name and yearning for monogrammed towels. A composite of many people was the here-and-now me: the baying hound, another girl who kept changing her mind, and especially, of all people, the Jean Genet character. Even the squabbling couple fitted in; I had certainly heard *that* fight before, and what made me feel seasick was that I was not one of these dreary, pathetic people, but both.

As morning approached, there were nightmare moments when I feared I couldn't hold on. I dreaded dissolving in a puddle of tears on the floor, just as the ex-liar—the minister, incidentally—had done. At the same time I felt an overwhelming sense of relief because I was all these different people and they were all me. It was as if, having finally dared to open Pandora's box, one found only oneself inside. Around midnight Saturday, I had thought that the play we were really enacting was Sartre's *No Exit* with its chilling message: "Hell is other people." But now in the misty hour of dawn it seemed to me instead that we were all of us in a dim, prehistoric cave, an ancient clan wrapped in animal skins and huddled around our council fire. Far from being atavistic or savage, this seemed to me a profoundly civilized scene. We were all human beings, sharing and savoring our common humanity, not out there in the jungle clawing and hacking each other to bits.

When the Sunday sun came up, I took my enormous breakfast out onto the front porch. The air smelled sweet and I felt immensely refreshed. It had been a great weekend. Most exhilarating was the knowledge that we had all come through the Marathon together—not merely that I had survived.

Broadway Show in a Theater of War

❧

Saigon

AIRLIFTING Mary Martin and the seventy-three members of her *Hello, Dolly!* troupe around the steaming jungle combat zones of South Vietnam last week at the very height of the war there raised all manner of exotic problems for the show folks and, I fear, a lot worse ones for the military. I went along too because although I have spent a lot of time around show business, I had certainly never visited a war. Nor until I saw it happen, had I ever dreamed that the two enterprises could coexist, the smaller show trouping around inside the bigger one, kicking up its high heels, packing and unpacking its crates of petticoats and painted scenery, while in the rice paddies all around it artillery rumbled and flights of armed helicopters hovered just above the proscenium. Often as Dolly sashayed her feathers and plumes around the sweltering, make-believe, crimson and gold interior of the Harmonia Gardens restaurant, she could watch real MEDEVAC rescue helicopters land their wounded and swiftly take off again right behind her audience's heads.

By the time the week ended, my admiration for all hands was vast, but I was particularly impressed by the unfailing

October 1965

grace with which the military handled a recreational project that, however noble in intent, must surely have disrupted their war. My own strictly personal problem during that mad, mad week as the choppers whirred and rattled, the Dollies capered, the delicate Vietnamese stared, and the servicemen roared with such force that curtain calls sounded like jet takeoffs, was somehow to convince myself that all the strange things happening here were not themselves part of a musical comedy, but actually part of a war.

The Barnum & Bailey notion that a full-fledged Broadway musical could be plopped into the middle of a combat zone and then trundled around it by armed convoy, could not, I felt sure, have possibly originated in the military mind. Indeed, I learned, the scheme hatched in the oriental brain of producer David Merrick. When he heard that the Russians had abruptly canceled out the Moscow portion of a State Department-sponsored *Dolly* tour just as his company was opening in Tokyo, it occurred to the stranded producer that another master showman, Lyndon Johnson, might like to book *Hello, Dolly!* into South Vietnam. According to Merrick, when he telephoned his offer to the White House, the occupant said, "Oh yes, that's the show that has my song in it!" and the new arrangements were made.

About two weeks later, now under military orders, the *Dolly* company left Tokyo in a drab, windowless troop transport. As we prepared to let down in Saigon, our escorting officer advised us that our arrival had been preceded by the most massive security precautions ever undertaken in that city, and that we would now make a "speed penetration landing to avoid picking up any small-arms fire." But even tilting down fast and backward into a real war, it was difficult for me to view the episode as anything but part of a road-show tour. When we landed, the door was yanked open, and out of the streaming tropical downpour on the airfield leaped a tanned, handsome general to plant a dashing kiss on Mary Martin's cheek. At the same time a flock of exquisite girls in graceful floor-length gowns and white gloves appeared out of the wet and started entwining fresh flower garlands around everybody's neck. A bit corny perhaps, but a socko opening number. Where else but in a musical comedy could one see flowing-haired girls singing "Hello, Dolly!" to chopper pilots on headsets as they hovered low over a bright green jungle? Where else see an impeccable oriental dignitary, Premier Ky, elegant in a starched white uniform, startled by an impulsive smooch from Miss Mary Martin of Weatherford, Texas? Another light-opera classic was the gala reception at the U.S. Embassy—where a string trio played, fans whirled, potted plants swayed, and suddenly "Some Enchanted Evening" boomed across the crowded room in a rich, schmaltzy baritone. The handsome soloist was Ambassador Lodge himself. Topping off all the rest, there was even a real moment at Nha Trang Air Base when, after much behind-the-scenes wire-pulling, we all watched a recently wounded rifleman unexpectedly reunited with his girlfriend, a dancer in the troupe. As the young couple embraced, everybody choked up, and Mary Martin spoke a perfect curtain line, "Dolly Levi *is* a matchmaker, after all."

As the week wore on, the two different worlds of the Army and Broadway became intertwined in ways that might have startled the Pentagon, but seemed jauntily appropriate in the field. Sometimes the Air Force borrowed *Dolly* microphones to dispatch pilots on urgent missions. At a press briefing it was solemnly announced, amid the rest of the battle news, that at 1600 hours Mary Martin would plant a tree. There were bits of low comedy, as when a sergeant serving as an amateur stagehand accidentally folded up a little dancer in a scenery flat; and there was a marvelous State Department man who kept asking, if this was *Hello, Dolly!* where was Louis Armstrong? Shortly before curtain time at Bien Hoa, General Westmoreland expressed his regrets to producer David Merrick that he would have to leave before the performance was over. He explained he had to fly to Hong Kong to greet

Congressman Rivers, chairman of the House Armed Services Committee. "I quite understand, General," said the producer. "You must deal with your angels just as I must deal with mine."

Despite all the high spirits, I continued to wonder whether all the problems and perils could be justified by the throat-stopping roars the show did evoke. I was inclined to think not, at least not in that particularly harrowing week of war. There are over 140,000 Americans in Vietnam, and I doubt that more than 12,000 were able to see the show. But from a long-range point of view I think that President Johnson's instinct for showmanship has again served him well. The *Dolly* tour taught the military a little about show business; more importantly, it may even result in attracting some small entertainment units to Vietnam, where they are very much needed. And the tour did much for the civilians involved in the operation. A doctor took a couple of *Dolly* girls and me on a helicopter hop to a tented field hospital. Another chopper landed just behind us, and when the *Dolly* girls saw the stretcher being lifted from it, they were suddenly scared about going into the hospital. "What should we say to them?" one girl asked the doctor.

"Don't worry," he answered, and just then we passed under the tent flap and saw eight bandaged, unconscious, naked bodies lying sweating on cots. They said it to us. Hello, Dolly. Hello, Vietnam.

I'd Know Him Anywhere

❧

HAVING spent most of the last month intensely watching Lyndon Johnson in a number of exotic, if not outlandish, situations—a muddy jungle, a golden throne, a Korean rice paddy, a kangaroo cookout—I should find it easier to visualize him now, especially in so familiar a setting as a hospital bed. But President-watching doesn't seem to work that way. The Presidency is an abstraction, but Mr. Johnson is a flesh-and-blood man.

Before the Asia tour I had never even seen him. The personal question that most preoccupied me during his entire whizzing gallop around the rim of the Pacific was: How much of what I am seeing will I be able to keep?

One way I tried to keep it was by scooping up every map, flag, press kit, speech, guidebook, travel folder, and souvenir offered us by the seven proud countries we visited. More than thirty pounds of this stuff still lies strewn about my living room, a thick mulch of official paper covering coffee table, couch, and piano top, and ornamented with the purple silk and yellow velvet armbands, the short snorters of special press badges, the delicate bit of gold filigree that got you into the Bangkok palace grounds, the heavy bronze souvenir medallion from the White House, the sandalwood menus, the kangaroo mittens, the Eskimo slippers, the carabao briefcase, and the

November 1966

lifetime pass on the Korean railroad. I am still reluctant to sort it all out and put it away, as if that simple act of housekeeping might somehow diminish the enormous dimensions of the trip. But though I superstitiously preserve this mulch, I have learned that the mind is able to "keep" an astonishing number of vivid impressions without recourse to notebooks or souvenirs.

Two hundred thousand New Zealanders had turned out to cheer the President. That bright, sunny morning in Wellington's Civic Square park the crowds were so immense that I could see in no direction but straight up, where wildly cheering people festooned every roof and window ledge. Suddenly the crowd opened up directly in front of me and there he was, prancing around the grassy oval like a prize show horse and flipping his fingers in the high, dainty, overhead waving one had seen so often on TV. Suddenly, amazingly, he flopped to his knees before a formal bed of bright red tulips and seized one slender stem in his big paw. It looked for one awful instant as if he intended to pick it, but he just buried his nose in the petals and sniffed deeply.

The next time I saw him, he was inside a very dark sheep-shearing shed. Cameramen were massed all over the railings and rafters, and you knew by the sudden noise and excitement when he had come in, even though you couldn't see a thing. Then a photographer standing on the fence right in front of me moved his foot, and there was the famous face again, brightly floodlit, framed in the black triangle of the cameraman's legs, peering narrowly down into a pen of live sheep.

Because of the enormous and ever-present crowds, one always saw the President either in these sudden, startling close-ups, or else in extreme long shots; there was no midde distance. Not all of the scenes were as corny as the tulips and the sheep. A few were scary, like the moment in Sydney when the crowds turned suddenly hostile, and our motorcade sped through a gauntlet of black confetti and black balloons. A few were funny—the grunting, tattooed Maori chief who disconcerted the Secret Service by brandishing a spear and sticking out his tongue at the President in a traditional tribal greeting; the garden club lady frantically waving at Lady Bird with a calla lily; the mother who slid her baby at the President across the top of his bubble-top limousine as if it were a poker chip. (LBJ slid it right back.)

And some were deeply moving. One day Johnson visited a remote hamlet in the sweltering Malaysian jungle. A tropical downpour was just ending as his helicopter clattered down, and children and scrawny chickens scattered in the mud while a native band beating on tom-toms came marching out of the jungle. After some brief ceremonies in appalling heat, LBJ stopped to shake hands with a group of village children. Seeing him standing there in the red mud amid the flocks of chickens and five-year-olds, I was very proud that the U.S. President had come to this place.

That moment was well along in the trip, and I felt I was seeing the President pretty clearly by then. In the beginning, I hadn't been able to see him at all. It wasn't a matter of optics, but a quirk of psychological "seeing"; over the seventeen days he literally emerged, like a photographic plate developing in the mind's eye.

I saw him for the first time ever in a receiving line in Honolulu. But though my notebook comments, "Grand-fatherly, almost grandmotherly," I can no longer dredge up the slightest personal recollection of that encounter.

The next day, I spent ten minutes with Mr. Johnson aboard Air Force One. But the embarrassing truth is that I have little direct memory of that encounter either. The astounding fact of being, except for two secretaries, alone with and about eighteen inches away from the President of the United States has blotted out everything else from my senses. I remember mostly the big brown face, the blinding Thai silk dressing gown, the powerfully direct manner and language: "Asia is where the action is. The Philippines is right in the center. I could throw a rock from Manila to Seoul."

185)

Seven countries later, the President and Mrs. Johnson walked stiffly and slowly down the flower-garlanded ramp at Kimpo Airport, Seoul. The cannon boomed and the jets in formation overhead trailed plumes of pink, lavender, green, blue, and yellow smoke, wrapping a giant rainbow around the whole bright scene. Now I am familiar enough with the sight of him, I thought, to see that he is finally growing tired.

The last time I saw him it was well past midnight in Alaska. We had all been crushed motionless for some time in the jam-packed hotel lobby when suddenly the Boy Scout band struck up an earsplitting "Hello, Lyndon!" and everybody began to yell. I didn't actually see him, but over the tops of a hundred heads a hat moved and a hand was flipping rapidly. That's him, I thought, I'd know him anywhere.

8

I Stand Up

Adventures of a Peeping Mom

A COUPLE of weeks ago I spent a day and a half in a dark mop closet at my daughter's school, staring into her kindergarten classroom through a hidden viewing window. I caught hell for it afterward from everybody except my daughter, whom I intend to keep unaware of my invasion of her privacy, at least until she is old enough to read this confession.

My daughter is not yet four. It was her first day in the new school and, I realize now, we were equally apprehensive. After I had delivered her to class, the school directress, who is a friend, casually offered me a key to the mop closet. Its viewing window is normally used to train student teachers without distracting the youngsters. From their side the children see only a big mirror on the wall.

I entered the closet, drew the window curtain, and saw my daughter seated at a small table directly facing and barely five feet from the mirror where I hid. Though I knew she couldn't see me, she seemed to be gazing right straight at me, grave and beautiful. In a cabinet at her elbow were new crayons, paper, paste, scissors, puzzles—all her special favorites. The children were free to select any equipment they wished, and all the other youngsters already were busily at work. I was eager to see what my daughter would do first.

She did nothing. She looked around, yawned occasionally, and that was it. She didn't touch crayons or paste, she didn't

March 1965

talk or smile or even cry. She didn't really look unhappy; she just looked as if she were casing the joint. Incredibly, this lively child sat there almost motionless for nearly six hours, and so, in mounting wonder, did I. When the pleasant-looking teacher spoke to her, she refused to answer. When a little boy drifted by and impulsively hugged her, she pushed his arm away. I felt heartbroken, embarrassed, angry, and proud in turn, and finally hypnotized, like some monstrous watcher at a human marineland.

When the teacher was on the far side of the room, a bigger girl cruised by my window, sharklike, and suddenly gave my daughter's hair a vicious tug. She barely flinched. I wanted to shout, to leap through the evil mirror like an avenging super-mother. But I didn't move. I even stayed frozen when the bully cruised back and tried to stick a finger up my daughter's nose. But the worst time of all was recess. Then all the children trooped noisily outside to the playground and the two of us were left absolutely alone, together but apart, for an eternal half hour.

When our mutual ordeals ended—hers of bravery, mine of cowardice—I picked her up at the school gate and inquired as casually as I could how she had liked school. She said, "Fine," and I redeemed my self-esteem slightly by letting the matter go at that.

It was at noon the next day, as I was back in the closet intently watching my daughter not eat lunch for the second time in a row, that I suddenly lost my nerve. It wasn't really the lunch that worried me. I was pretty sure her appetite would return, along with her smile and the use of her limbs, as soon as she got used to things, and it all has. What worried me was how badly I was hooked. Staring at the unfed child and the undrunk glass of milk, I'd caught myself idly figuring how to fit regular daily visits to this fascinating place into my own busy routine. Overnight the uncomfortable mop closet had become as seductive as an opium den. I fled.

Though it seemed wise to avoid the mop closet until I was

sure I'd kicked the peeping habit, I did talk a lot about the place to friends. Mention of the secret window triggered violent reactions. Perfectly reasonable people turned purple and accused me of everything from creeping big brotherism to peeping momism, from invasion of my daughter's privacy to destruction of her human dignity. The harshest critics said that I was wreaking irrevocable psychological havoc on a defenseless child. Others felt that while peeping momism does no harm to the peeped-upon, it inevitably corrupts the watcher in the closet.

Though shaken, I thought the uproar quite silly. For one thing, I'm not sure a small child has much right of privacy; that's just one of the rotten facts of life about being three years old. But what was most baffling was the intensity of everybody's outrage.

It took a news report from Washington on the latest electronic bugging devices, including the transistorized cocktail olive, to remind me that snooping, legal and otherwise, is a major obsession of our age. In the era of the master fingerprint file, the televised bank robbery, the watched YMCA toilet, and the bugged martini, we are naturally supersensitive to peeking and fearful of entrapment.

Excesses of snooping are of course loathsome, but it seems to me they are a natural outgrowth of our age's real preoccupation, which is not snooping, but fact. Mass communications have accustomed us to massive doses of fact on every conceivable subject, yet the daily barrage of detailed documentary reports seems only to leave us panting for more. Every reporter knows that the more detailed facts you manage to cram into your report, the more absolutely certain you are to have someone say: Great job, but tell me, what is Lyndon Johnson (or Liz, or Mississippi, or smoking marijuana) *really like?*

Journalists themselves are scarcely immune to this obsession with what things are *really like.* No wonder I found a day in that mop closet hopelessly seductive. They should post the place: Journalists and anxious mothers enter at own risk. Still, now that I know what the opium is made of, I plan to drop by the mop closet from time to time with a free heart. People-watching, I claim, can be as innocent and pleasurable as bird-watching and even more instructive. Far from being sinister, there is something of great value, as well as pleasure, in learning passively to observe someone you love, especially a small child, without interfering or imposing one's own powerful presence. I have learned, for example, that my daughter is able to fend for herself in her world far better than I had thought and that she very much enjoys the opportunity. We now try to give her more independence at home as well as at school, and she appears to be blooming.

The only danger in people-watching is the terrible temptation to butt in, to really turn into supermother, to smash the glass and spoil the game. Pretending to be a fly on the wall is good training for anxious mothers because it places an absolute moral burden of nonintervention on the fly.

My Friend in Watts

W

WHY do the finest flowers sometimes sprout from the worst dungheaps? This puzzle is what first took me to Watts, California, two years before the riots there. The flower in question was a young man named Stan Sanders, Watts born and raised, who had just been selected as one of America's first two Negro Rhodes scholars. What interested me most about Stan was that the more I came to know about him, the more I began to suspect that his extraordinary string of accomplishments and great sweetness of nature had been achieved not so much in spite of Watts as in some strange way because of it. Although the ghetto damages most inhabitants, it spares a few and sometimes casts them far higher up the beach than they might otherwise expect, and this seemed to be what had happened in Stan's case. He had been president of his junior and senior high schools in Watts. By the time I met him as a college senior, he was the wildly popular student body president of Whittier College, and a small college All-American football player. Indeed he had just turned down a $13,000 offer from the Chicago Bears in order to accept what he considered the better offer from the Rhodes committee. He seemed able to move back and forth between the all-white world of Whittier and the all-black world of Watts with particular grace and skill, his sober Mayan-mask features exploding often

August 1965

and freely into an amazing Walt Disney smile. His special taste and talent was for leadership; his idol was Gandhi; he was thinking of becoming a Quaker, and his ambition was to study law and then return to Watts to practice and to enter politics.

In the six months before he went to England, Stan and I had many long talks. I wanted to write something about Stan and his family and Watts that would also make a comment about American Negro life today. Even without the crowning ornament of Stan, the Sanderses are an unusual clan. Like many newcomers to Watts, Stan's parents came there as Southern field hands. Unlike most, they stayed. Stan's father drove a city garbage truck for twenty-eight years, and Stan was born in the front bedroom of the tiny bungalow where the Sanderses still live. In 1952 the family's oldest boy, Big Ed, became Olympic heavyweight boxing champion. Then, when Stan was twelve, Ed turned pro and was killed in the ring. A few years later, Stan's sister married Earl Battey, All-Star catcher for the Minnesota Twins. When Mr. Sanders retired at sixty-five, he enrolled in the sixth grade at the same Watts school where Stan had been president. Stan's mother went there too, and when I first knew the family, three generations of Sanderses used to sit around the same big dining table together doing their homework. What fascinated me most about these people was that, under the most deprived and unlikely of circumstances, the Sanderses came closer than any other family I knew—white or black—to embodying the old-fashioned American Dream. Family stability, warmth, closeness, poverty, hard work, and individual success were all represented at that table in truly staggering amounts. The central reason for this, I concluded, was that these were among the last people in America who still believed in the Dream in a totally uncynical way. Cynical myself, I sometimes thought that only the parents' lack of education could make such wholehearted belief possible. At the same time it was clear that the staunchness of the belief was what was making the Dream come true.

(194

Alas, I never published the story. On paper, I could not make the Sanders family come alive. But over the next two years we all kept in touch. Stan, I knew, was getting a full European education—letters arrived from Paris cafés and Danish beaches as well as from Oxford cloisters—but I couldn't readily picture him in any of these places. In my mind's eye he was always where I'd first seen him in Watts: sitting in the back of an open convertible, waving and grinning and leading a parade from Los Angeles City Hall down the main street of Watts to celebrate Stan Sanders Day. The sidewalks were lined with cheering citizens, and the festivities wound up with a sort of Stan Sanders, This Is Your Life pageant in the high school auditorium. The Day, as he always called it, was certainly the biggest thing that ever happened to Stan and, until last week, I suspect it was also the biggest thing that ever happened to Watts.

All morning long on Friday the thirteenth, when the riots began to look really bad, I tried to call the Sanders house, but the line was busy. (Stan had returned to Los Angeles for a few weeks to see his family before starting Yale Law School in the fall.) Finally I reached his sister, Margaret Ann Battey, who told me she was keeping her three children indoors and that Stan had gone off to City Hall to see what he could do.

That morning the burning began. Stan first saw the flames from the freeway as he was driving back home from his fruit-less trip to the Mayor's office. "Shana, don't come down here!" he shouted on the phone. "Watts is burning. The authorities are saying: Let the niggers burn themselves up!" Then he faltered, cursed, and hung up.

We met the next morning in neutral territory, the lobby of a downtown hotel. Stan was still wearing the same dapper "ice cream" suit I'd helped pick out before he went away to Oxford, but it looked filthy, and he told me he'd been on the street in the middle of the riot all night, trying to help some Negro newsmen friends. Stan himself had regained his charac-teristic Buddha-like composure, his slow, forty-eight-beat athlete's pulse seemingly back to normal after the previous day's emotional outburst and the night of violence that followed. I read him something from my two-year-old notebook: "There are degrees of being a Negro. I don't think like a Negro but like a human being. If somebody wants to reject me on the basis of color, that's his problem, not mine." Do you still feel that way, I asked.

"I feel like a schizophrenic," he replied. The riot had made him realize that he might at any moment literally be forced to choose between the white world and the black, and there could be no question what his choice would be. Stan also felt deep despair. "In Europe, sometimes, I used to have a fantasy of a riot at home—Watts has been due for this a long time—but I always imagined myself quelling it. Last night I found I was just as helpless as before I left."

But I sensed the real change in Stan when I asked him what it felt like to see rubble filling the same streets that had contained the Stan Sanders Day parade. "I find the Day and the riots absolutely compatible," he said. "A community takes pride in things it has achieved. Then it vents its hatred against the thing it despises." At the height of the violence, he went on, he found himself joyously speaking the nitty-gritty Negro argot he hadn't used since junior high, and despite the horrors of the night, this morning he felt a strange pride in Watts. "As a riot," he told me, "it was a masterful performance. I sense a change there now, a buzz, and it tickles. For the first time people in Watts feel a real pride in being black. I remember when I first went to Whittier, I worried that if I didn't make it there, if I was rejected, I wouldn't have a place to go back to. Now I can say: 'I'm from Watts.'"

A Valkyrie at the Beauty Ranch

🌷

I SOLD out again recently to something I have been trying to avoid most of my adult life.

Not many Monday mornings ago, I was one of a column of twenty ladies skipping at top speed, barefooted, around the edge of a swimming pool in time to the spirited whistle of the "Colonel Bogey" march. We were identically clad in pink sweat suits, and we were all overwrought, out of breath, out of shape, and in every way a horrible contrast to our leader, a flaxen Viking with a Miss Universe smile and thews like Paavo Nurmi. She led us thrice high-stepping briskly around the pool and thence into an open-air gym where we were confronted with a rumbling panzer division of heavy-duty reducing machines, all the more menacing for being painted baby pink.

Collapsing onto a pink wrestling mat, I wondered what I was doing here, although of course I knew perfectly well. This was a health resort, a beauty ranch—all right, a fat farm. I had wanted to visit such a place for a long time, but had never before felt fat enough, tired enough, rich enough, and brave enough all in the same week. My bravery now was bolstered by the presence of two old friends, who had been coming here happily for several years. But though I thought I knew what to expect, in the quivering flesh a fat farm turns out to be full of surprises, the first of which is how much that flesh can be made to endure.

November 1965

Each day was regulated by a gold-embossed tag in the shape of a clockface, which told us where to be when, and I have preserved my seven-day collection of clocks, in the same spirit, I imagine, that surgery veterans keep their kidney stones in a bottle. My Monday tag shows that after the wake-up calisthenics, I staggered through bouts of steam and massage; took an ancient Sumerian bath (in a shallow stone sarcophagus filled with cold water); did some Javanese water exercises (standing in a shoulder-deep pool, one attempts to do things under water with an absolutely unsinkable water-polo ball); attended a spot-reducing class (those grim pink machines); enjoyed an herbal wrap (steaming linen shrouds wrung out in boiling tea); and then celebrated a two-hour ritual inadequately called "beauty," in which one was first outfitted with hot mittens, matching electric socks, and eyepads, and then given a languorous facial in what seemed to be snow, bear grease, and crème de menthe. After beauty that day my clock reads, "Yoga, jazz exercise; vapor room; cocktails, dinner." But had I known in advance the true meaning of the last two items, I would have eaten the facial. Dinner was a meat loaf made from ground-up cucumbers, and the "cocktail"—cruel jest—was potassium broth.

That night, lying sleepless in my expensive pink room, I wondered how I would survive the week. It wasn't just that I hate exercise; I also hate groups, I have no team spirit, I love privacy. The prospect of a week's confinement in desert isolation with twenty overweight women of middle age and up, all but two of whom I presumed to be idle, vain, silly females—the gaggle of us to be tended by hearty Norse goosegirls of iron good cheer, and the whole absurdity to be sustained by nothing but vain dreams of youth and hearty quaffs of potassium broth—was enough to curdle my tired blood. In addition to its disagreeable similarities to a girls' boarding school, the place reminded me of two other institutions I can't stand—fancy beauty parlors and health food stores. Lying there helpless in the predawn silence, I could

(198

only vow, as I have done before in other hopeless fixes, "They'll never get me!"

But of course they did. By the third day I had fallen magically into the spirit of the place, skipping around the pool after my Viking like a Valkyrie, sloshing in the Sumerian tubs, and looking forward sensually to my siesta in the electric socks. What really hooked me, saved me—and at the same time constituted my sellout—was sheer herd instinct, the very side of my nature I keep trying to suppress. In adversity, the pesky, archaic thing reasserted itself. Not only did I find myself sharing confidences and giggling like a schoolgirl with my own two friends; soon I was getting terribly involved with other ladies, the same I had dismissed as just a bunch of silly, rich, vain women. Inside our strange, looking-glass world, the sharp, brief glimpses into their lives on the "outside" were enchanting, touching, and sometimes hair-raising. Part of me has always yearned to be mistress of a grand establishment, but when one new friend told me what it was like to live amid eleven servants, I felt the back of my neck prickle. Talk about privacy! I was delighted by the woman who asked me my name in the steam room. When I told her she exclaimed, "Really? That's the name of my horse!" And I shall never forget honest, sixtyish Mrs. Thatcher. To demonstrate how long one minute really is, our yoga instructor had told us each to lie flat on the floor, close our eyes, and when we thought a minute had passed, raise our hand. "And no fair counting to sixty. That's cheating," he warned. We all flunked miserably except Mrs. Thatcher, who said airily, "I just imagined I was boiling my husband's three-minute breakfast egg, but I made it only one-third done."

By week's end I found myself exercising like a demented Rockette, and when we finally got our lavender report cards, I learned I had lost four and a half pounds. More important, I was so exhilarated, so positively gingered up, I felt in imminent danger of fizzing.

This extreme carbonation has now passed, and the four and

a half pounds are back too (though not, thank heaven, in the same places). But my backache is gone, and the four and a half pounds will be easy to lose again. Indeed, I had already made a tentative reservation to take care of that next year when, just this morning, our group picture finally arrived in the mail. It makes me feel quite sentimental. There we are, all dressed alike in rumpled pink shorts, squinting in the sun and standing, sitting, and kneeling in a carefully composed group shot. It looks as if an old album photograph from my childhood in summer camp had been retouched by Dorian Gray. Slightly off to one side in our picture, in the camp counselor spot, stands our Viking. Inspecting her cool perfection, I find I don't feel sentimental about her at all. Good news, that. The herd instinct is part of me, I am forced to admit. But as long as I don't choke up over that Viking, I am at least not a total sellout.

Unaccustomed as I Am . . .

❦

I AM, God help me, about to do it for the fifth time. My hands, I know, will be wet and my mouth dry. There will even be an actual bumping inside my chest as I scrape back my chair and walk unsteadily to the podium. "Thank you very much" (gulp . . . weak smile) "and good evening, ladies and gentlemen."

My horror of stages, speeches, spotlights, and footlights is old stuff. I am a born spectator. My natural habitat is the audience. I know my place, and it is not in the spotlight. It is back up there in the snug, anonymous dark.

There is only one vantage point in the theater that is more delectable to me than a back-row seat, and that is a stool in the wings. From that most privileged backstage perch, one can observe both the performance taking place onstage and the response it draws forth from the audience. One is in touch with each, yet a part of neither. As a journalist, I have been permitted to hang around a lot of backstages—at the circus, in a turmoil of tinsel and shouts and beasts and satin and feathers; at Broadway openings and Balinese dance concerts; at ballet pandemoniums and gaudy Las Vegas girl shows. Wings-watching has always induced in me a scarily omnipotent feeling, akin to playing God.

I first emerged from the wings in a walnut shell towed by two mice. It was a fourth-grade production of *Thumbelina*,

May 1967

and my mortifying costume was a leaf. Merciful obscurity closed in after that until the time came to make a speech at my eighth-grade graduation. By then I was burdened with twenty pounds of overweight, a mouthful of braces, and a broken leg. The event was so traumatic that for the next twenty years I stayed resolutely off the stage, refusing to take part in school plays, team athletics, dance contests, or campus politics. I even got my college diploma by mail. Though my wedding took place in the relative privacy of my parents' living room, I would have preferred the even greater anonymity of city hall.

For years I refused all invitations to participate in panel discussions, disk-jockey interviews, political rallies, awards ceremonies, or tree plantings. I never asked questions from the floor at lectures or volunteered to help the magician in the nightclub. At raffles, half of me hoped I didn't have the lucky number.

The carrot that finally coaxed me out of the wings was, of all things, a journalism award. No acceptance speech, they said, no award. O vanity, vanity! I said I'd be there.

But there was something more to it than that. I really started speaking for the same reason that I stopped smoking. I was ashamed of myself. It was time to grow up. But the older one gets, it seems, the harder that is to do.

As my D day approached, I retreated. Friends had rallied round with all sorts of advice, mostly contradictory. Don't be afraid to write it out. Read it. Memorize it. Put it on cards. Speak it off the cuff. Start funny. Start dull—an early joke lets them off the hook of curiosity. Turn from side to side so they can all see you. Find one nice face in the audience and tell it all to him. Get a new dress. Get a little drunk.

By the afternoon of the speech, trying to follow all this advice at once, I sat stupefied with terror in my room in the hotel where the banquet was to be held. My new gown hung on the back of the door, flowers and telegrams began to arrive. Were they condolences? Had I already died? Set out along the desk beside the typewriter were black coffee, tranquilizers, whiskey, and an enormous dessert. I swallowed first one thing and then the other, striving for equilibrium like Alice nibbling from her mushroom. The black coffee fed the writer; the whiskey nourished the coward; the ice cream was for the scared child, and the tranquilizers—something new—were my hole card. I barely remember going downstairs to the hotel ballroom, or climbing the dais, or eating the dinner, or anything at all until I felt my wet palms gripping the smooth sides of the lectern and heard my own weird, oddly magnified voice rumble out over the crowd.

I was most unprepared for my own total unpreparedness: I didn't know where to look, where to put my hands, where to pitch my voice, when to pause, when to smile. To be *that* unknowing rarely happens to an adult; it gave me a giddy feeling; nothing to do but push on.

After a few moments I heard faint laughter. I was not quite conscious of it at first, but then it came again a bit stronger, until I was sure I heard it, and then as I was reading, I began to wait for it, and to make spaces in sentences for it, to enjoy it, and finally to play with the words and with the audience, to swoop and glide and describe arabesques with all the nutty abandon of Donald Duck on ice skates.

Success. Triumph. Waves of applause. The night came to a kind of crescendo Andy Hardy finish that I have never been able to recapture. In the next three speeches I was nearly as scared as the first time, but not nearly as good. But I am going to try it again. I am getting to know the ropes.

A good speech must be written out. In speaking, the pen is still more important than the tongue. But the rules of speech-writing are different; a different sort of carpentry is required. Adjectives are more important in speaking than in writing. The very weakness of writing, which is adjectives, is the strength of speaking. Repetition is important, too; the ear has a short memory. When you listen to a speech, the words literally go in one ear and out the other. So your main point ought to come early in the speech, and there should be continual reference back to it. Make jokes, but make them slowly; don't be afraid to stretch them out. Slowness followed by sudden acceleration is good, too. So is comedy juxtaposed to sudden solemnity, or vice versa. In speaking, you can really play an audience in a way a writer never can. A speech is not a lecture. The object is not to get points over; it is to try to make people feel something. That is a terribly interesting challenge for a writer—to try to intensify with voice and delivery what you used to try to accomplish merely with words.

I am becoming fascinated with the similarities and the differences between the two modes. Though speaking is still not fun, I want very much now to learn to do it better. And I enjoy the applause. Irving Berlin was right: There is no business like show business. Among other things, an occasional show-off trip to the podium turns out to be the perfect condiment to spice the introvert writer's life.

A Big Mistake in London

🌷

I DID something in London recently that one should simply never do: I contrived to be invited to tea by a favorite author whom I had never met. It is not visiting writers in their native habitat that is intrinsically so harmful. The mistake lies in crowding in too close to someone you have admired extravagantly from a long way off. As a general rule, fans and idols should always be kept at arm's length, the length of the arm to be proportionate to the degree of sheer idolatry involved. Don't take a Beatle to lunch. Don't wait up to see if the Easter Bunny is real. Just enjoy the egg hunt.

London is advertised as the swingingest city in the world, and it is certainly true that once you get caught in the fizzed-up, urbane atmosphere of the place, all sorts of implausible notions become thinkable. One evening, for example, I found myself at a hunt ball. Descending the staircase in my rented silver ball gown, I felt like a revolving chandelier, and the chandelier feeling lingered long after the ball was over. In the next days I did many other things I don't do at home: made a wild bet on a race; walked in a fountain; tried to play the bagpipes; flirted with the monocled eye of the second richest man in the world; designed the world's first hamster-fur miniskirt, and waited three days for an appointment with a clairvoyant.

My favorite author is probably not yours. I believe he has

April 1966

written only two books, and neither of them is widely known. But when I read them a couple of years ago, they seemed unmistakably custom-written for me, "personalized" for me in the same sense that tie-clasp manufacturers use that hideous word. One book, a sort of novel, is precisely the sort of novel I would wish to write. The second book, vaguely autobiographical, even succeeded in making me feel that it was just the autobiography I might write if I had been born a man and had lived this man's life. I realize this may sound foolish; perhaps any infatuation is at bottom unexplainable.

When, one afternoon, a chance acquaintance disclosed that my Favorite Author was at present in London and could readily be called upon, I ignored the lessons of a lifetime and once more set off in pursuit of the Easter Bunny.

Our appointment was for exactly five o'clock. In the taxi I remembered something that happened more than fifteen years ago to a young friend of mine named Russell Hemenway, who had gone to Paris to be a writer. Late one night in a little café, my friend saw a big, bearded man alone at the bar. Ernest Hemingway! Overwhelmed by equal parts hero worship and gin, my friend allowed himself to approach the solitary figure. "Sir," he said, "my name is Russell Hemenway. I majored in you at Dartmouth, and I've read every word you ever wrote, and, well, I just wanted to say hello. My name is Russell HEMENWAY."

The Favorite Author lumbered to his feet, stuck out a paw, and said, "How do you do? All my life, people have asked me if I'm related to you."

The taxi stopped. I pushed the downstairs buzzer. A bicycle was parked inside the front door, a cap hung over the handlebars. "Come on up," a voice shouted down the stairwell. "Be with you in a moment." I don't remember my author's voice, nor even what he looked like beyond a dim impression of height and horn-rimmed spectacles. But I recall in great detail the room we talked in. It was high-ceilinged and totally empty of furniture except for a narrow daybed and a desk. There was

(206

no desk chair. A bare light bulb hung from the ceiling, pigeons wheeled and flapped in the afternoon sunshine outside the big uncurtained bay window, and a folding bed printed with red cabbage roses and a small pile of bedding were neatly stacked on the floor near the door. Tea was brewed, I perched on the daybed, the author fetched a chair from another room and leaned back expansively. "Well!" he said.

Though our conversation was quite ordinary, I remember the next hour as one of the most acutely uncomfortable I have ever spent. What made it worse was that he seemed so maddeningly at ease. Proof that my visit was in no way a put-on but was in fact a genuine literary fan call, no more, no less, was impossible for me to proffer, even if he had asked it, which he did not. As we talked, it seemed to me we were playing an extremely elaborate game, probably Japanese, in which players wear medieval armor and ornate masks. But I didn't know what the game was. Rules, penalties, stakes, and tactics were all equally mysterious.

The trouble, I think now, was that I knew his books so intimately I presumed I knew the man. But my author parried well, refusing to permit unwarranted familiarity. Our conversation did not mesh properly. I heard with mounting horror my own voice chattering on about his books and what I saw in them; heard his noncommittal, periodic replies, just barely enough to keep the conversation going. "Oh, yes? Oh yes." Half rabbi, half myna bird. "Oh yes."

In my emotion-charged state of mind his most commonplace remarks set off immense reverberations, until it seemed to me that overtones of this utterly banal talk had begun to clang through the oddly bare room. My head teemed with impossibly personal questions. Why no furniture? Was he hungry? On dope, perhaps? Had he just moved in; was he just moving out? Why the folded bed with roses? Had a mistress deserted? Was a dead lady newly bricked into the wall? Had he committed an unspeakable crime perhaps, or suffered an unbearable wound? There was no way to find out.

I rose to go. "I have been around awhile," I said. "And I really know better than to drop in cold on Albert Schweitzer or Marilyn Monroe."

"Then you do understand," he said, smiling warmly for the first and last time. I understood, but I could not help myself. And when he directed me toward a taxi stand, saying, "There are two ways to go. The short way is the quick way, but the long way is the sure way," I felt the old vibrations starting up again.

I cried in the taxi all the way down the Bayswater Road. The reason, I suppose, was some sort of overflowing of emotion not expressed. The acute phase of melancholy was over by the time I reached my hotel, but many other reverberations of that visit will stay with me a long time. The loudest clang of all is to realize that, like every other misadventure I have deliberately embarked on with wide-open eyes, now that it is over I am very glad I did it.

The Surprises of the Mail

NOTHING gives one the same small, dependable thrill as looking through the morning mail and spotting amid the circulars, the requests for funds, the bills, the stuff addressed to "occupant," and the magazine renewal forms, one crisp envelope, covered with stamps, bordered with airmail stripings, and addressed not by machine but in human handwriting, it scarcely matters whose. A personal letter puts a fine little zing in a day. Even on the blackest, most desperate of mornings—and this past week certainly has had its share—I know I can count on two or three minutes of unalloyed high hopes as I make my way down to the mailbox.

Letters are expectation packaged in an envelope. Perhaps that is why all the attendant paraphernalia of letter writing is pleasing, too—creamy notepaper, sealing wax, broad-nib pens, colored inks, intricate calligraphy, crests and monograms, codes and homemade hieroglyphics and airmail flimsies, and fancy desk sets and electric typewriters. Stationery stores soothe me in a way that Muzak never can.

I rue the invention of the telephone not only because I hate the black ever-jangling thing for its own sake. I also regret the decline it has caused in personal correspondence. A handwritten, personal letter has become a genuine modern-day luxury, like a child's pony ride.

The best letter to receive, I think, is also the most pleasing

June 1967

one to write. That is the impulsive kind, the one dashed off on an airplane, scrawled on a paper napkin or a torn-off scrap of envelope. It contains sudden thought, a gush of love, a wild opinion, some urgent need to communicate with a particular other living being. So when the impulse strikes, do it, scribble it down, throw it in an envelope, and mail it off. If necessary, cork it in a bottle and drop it over the side.

My desk is a large plain table piled with books, papers, file folders, mailing supplies, photographs, bills, letters, and so on, each tottering stack lidded with some kind of heavy weight. But in all the desk-top welter, nothing weighs more than an unanswered letter from a friend. I have quite a few of these right now, and I think the only rule to follow when your desk top achieves this level of backed-up clutter is this: Never let an unanswered letter from one friend inhibit you from striking up new correspondence with someone else.

In all correspondence, private or professional, tone of voice seems to be the most important thing. The voice that you hear as you read a letter always seems to be the other person's quintessential voice. If you love the person, you hear only his purest and most lovable qualities as you read. If you already dislike him, the letter becomes further evidence of his unattractiveness. Probably the papery abstraction of a letter permits the reader to impute to the writer whatever qualities the reader is already listening for. This strange polarizing effect is both the weakness of letter communication and the reason why correspondence, especially love letters, seems so pellucid compared to the ambiguities of real life.

Despite the old cautionary warning never to put it in writing, I would say always put it in writing. I think this rule holds especially true for love letters, the nation's lawyers to the contrary. In matters of love, something a lot worse than putting it in writing is not even putting it in writing. Not long ago I read the story of an Ohio woman who had died a recluse in a shabby home for the aged. When lawyers went to her last known residence, a large house in which she had lived alone save for six dogs, they found a locked closet and, on its top shelf, a cardboard shoe box containing over two hundred and fifty passionate love letters from Warren G. Harding. This was certainly the most interesting thing I had read in a long time about President Harding.

Saved-up letters age like wine in cellars. But it is more difficult to judge when old love letters are ripe for opening. Like wine, they tend to go flat when kept too long. On the top shelf of my closet I have long kept a packet of cherished old letters in a hatbox and another in a red bag. This month, in the course of a giant housecleaning in preparation for moving to a new home, I opened the mildewed hatbox. There were only dusty banalities inside, and I threw them out. I am not going to throw out the red bag. But I am not going to open it, either. Perhaps I never will. For the truth of old love letters, like the old loves themselves, is that they exist not in the bag but in the recollection. Exposure to the present, to the pitiless, naked eye of now, spoils them. Like an unwrapped pharaoh, they crumble to dust.

Although I have been dashing off impulse letters for some time, it is only recently—since beginning to write this column—that I have begun to receive them in any quantity. I read them all. Partly it is the writer's need for feedback. Is anybody out there listening? Partly, I have become hooked on the column mail for its own sake. Letter reading has a lot in common with beachcombing. You sift your way pleasantly through a great deal of unremarkable stuff, but the effort is worth it for the occasional unexpected find: the high school sweetheart, the dire astrological forecast, the invitation to an Irish castle, the long lost relative, the snarl of hate, the proposal of marriage, the explosive laugh.

In my personal, as opposed to professional, correspondence, I long ago learned that trying to extrapolate the man from his letters is a dangerous business. People in the flesh are a lot more complicated than they appear on the page, which is one of the attractions but also one of the shortcomings of carrying on a prolonged correspondence. But though I know perfectly well this time how perilous it is to invent a dummy author to fit the words and the style of the person on the page, once in a while the temptation is irresistible. I refer, of course, to my best beachcombing find, my prize fan letter, the one that dropped out of my office mail this morning and triggered all these remarks. It arrived on pink paper in a tiny envelope from some people I had never heard of:

Announcing the arrival of our new daughter

NAME: Shana Alexandra

DATE: May 24—10:18 A.M.

WEIGHT: 4 lbs. 10 oz.—18″

HAPPY PARENTS: Sam and Carole Clester.

Underneath, the mother had written, "We admire your writing so well that we decided your name was good enough for our first child. We think it is a very beautiful name, which only befits a very beautiful child."

If they don't sign them, I don't read them—that's my rule of thumb. A while ago an Illinois judge did sign his name to this:

> *Dear (?) Miss Alexander,*
> *Surely you don't really think you are passing your cute, slick little prejudicial blurbs off on the public as anything approaching objective commentary, do you? . . . The bile rises in my throat whenever I read your snide, petty hatred.*

I'd just as soon not hear anything more from the judge, but I hope very much that some day I will hear from Shana Alexandra again.

Take Your Hand off My Pulse

❦

I VOTE self-shrouded in monk's cloth: That happens to be the fabric that curtains the voting booths in my particular polling place. Other voters face their own moments of truth behind green baize, homespun, or hopsacking but, symbolically anyway, monk's cloth is best suited to this election year. If green baize invites a gamble, and sackcloth whispers atonement, monk's cloth suggests that austere scrupulosity of choice that the possibilities offered us in 1968 seemed most particularly to demand.

Everyone knows by now just how scrupulous were the choices we finally made. Everyone but me, that is—the old predicament of the journalist on a weekly deadline. The writer's present is the reader's past. Locked inside this prison cell of time, the temptation is to manufacture fudge. But I am sick to death of fudge. Often during the closing weeks of the political campaign I have felt myself drowning in a sea of the sticky stuff. Hedges, quibbles, cavils, boggles; pussyfoots, sidesteps, and straddles; begged questions, split hairs, and enough other assorted cop-outs to make a massive chocolate tide. Fudge from candidates is, at least, traditional. It was the huge outflow of candied statistics from the pollsters and their computers that became so cloying at the end. There were house-to-house polls, telephone polls, TV polls, postcard polls,

November 1968

coupon polls, newspaper polls, street-corner polls. And they asked questions covering everything from politics to trading stamps.

In all the fudge I found but two walnuts, the first being the well-buried statistic that, this year, growing numbers of Americans are just plain refusing to answer the questions. That brilliant tactic had not occurred to me. Pulse-takers habitually scry the tastes of 200 million people from samples of two thousand or less, so I've never held much hope of being polled myself. But in the unlikely event that some patient little man with an armful of graph paper ever did come knocking on my door, I had planned to weave for him the fanciest tangle of lies I could think of. I realize now that such an attitude is childish; a simple door-slam on the foot is the mature voter's response.

The second walnut was bigger. A poll on polls, taken by the Minneapolis *Tribune*, shows that 45 percent of people don't believe that polls are accurate anyway. I agree. In fact, I suspect the Minneapolis poll itself is off. Poll-takers constantly have to fight their own human, nonstatistical natures, and I have been delighted to learn that they frequently lose. Lou Harris had to be eased out the door by the Kennedys when he grew too fond of JFK to do a truly impartial job.

I don't believe in the polls for lots of other reasons. Canvassers cheat. People are quixotic. But even if all the techniques were foolproof, I would still want the polls to err. For one thing the imp of perversity is in serious danger of becoming extinct today, which would be a pity. Accordingly I root against UNIVAC on election night. I boo Brinks and cheer the bank robbers. A mere sexual hangup, perhaps? It is certainly true that no woman wants to be predictable to any man, let alone to Dr. Gallup. One of the most infuriating lines in marital warfare is the exultant cockcrow, "I knew exactly what you were going to do—*and you did it!*" Conversely, a few compliments beat the baritone murmur, "But you're not at *all* what I expected!"

But the real reason that I am against the polls is that I

fiercely dislike being told what I am going to do. I resent it not as a woman, but as a human being. It makes me suspect I may be being programmed. As the listings of everybody's political preferences according to age, race, education, income, geography, mental health, and so on, begin to pile up into that statistical alp—well-buttressed by the wondrous system of hedges and demurrers—I begin to feel insulted. I refuse to roost in anybody's pigeonhole. The pollsters' crystal ball aimed at me in my cloistered voting booth comes to seem the subtlest, and hence the most obscene, kind of invasion of privacy.

"There is only one of ME," I want to shout out to peepers Gallup, Harris & Co. Anybody who wants to know what I am like, and likely to do, is going to have to make a special trip over here to find out. I am me, and uniquely myself. Indeed, my own singularity is more and more the raft I cling to whenever I feel in danger of being swamped by our computerized, dehumanized shipwreck of society. As I hug hard to the floating plank that is me, it occurs to me that millions of others must be in the same state of mind. Perhaps hundreds of millions.

Politicians are unique, too, or at least they ought to try to be. And politicians who listen *too hard* to the polls, ears aquiver for feedback from the fickle electorate, are unable to hear themselves think. After a while they seem to stop trying. The bizarre political sequences of 1968 offer us several classic examples of such self-induced deafness. George Romney's decision to quit in New Hampshire was the very first time in American political history that a major presidential candidate withdrew from the race on the basis of public opinion polls. And that—as we all know now—was only the beginning.

Who did win all the elections, after all? How I wish I knew as I sit here typing in my cell, composing this manifesto in invisible ink, this note to be corked in a bottle and thrown over the wall of time's prison to those of you who are happily walking around out there in the present, knowing how it all came out.

You can guess what the note says, of course. If not, let me save you the trouble of heating the ink, cracking the code. It says: "They'll never fold, spindle, or mutilate me!"

9

McCarthy's Trojan Horse

🌷   🌷

🌷

Introduction

🌷

You'll have to write it as a novel. . . . Nobody would
believe the truth.

EUGENE MCCARTHY
September, 1968

Now I think they will. They will believe in 1970 what they
could not believe then. For 1968 was a special year, an
earthquake year. A Revolution happened in America, and we
are not the same country now the year has ended that we
were before it began. In this year the country changed and the
people changed, and the people are not as they were before it
began, either.

Perhaps the first paradox of the illimitable number of paradoxes that buzz like swarming flies of Fate around the silver-
gray-ghost persona of Eugene McCarthy is that the man who
fueled and guided, inspirited and embodied the change—the
nearly invisible man who led the Revolution by appearing not
to lead it—did not himself change at all.

No, that was the second paradox. The first paradox about
Senator McCarthy is the constant illusion that he is both there
and not-there. What is most noticeable about him is his invisi-
bility. We met for the first time five years ago in the White
House at a formal state dinner, put on by Lyndon Johnson for
the King of Morocco, potentate-to-potentate. I seem to remember every snowflake that fell on my hired limousine,

219)

every silvery fanfare, each flower and flutter and flash in this entire glittering evening, save one. Senator McCarthy was the host at my table during dinner, but he is just a recollected gray space, a blank, in an evening of red, white, and blue pomp.

Yet our second meeting, a modest lunch with my mother in a Beverly Hills restaurant, is as sharp-etched in my memory as a steel engraving. The club sandwiches, what we ate, what was said, tones of voice, quips, hands moving over the tablecloth—each detail is vivid still.

McCarthy remarked on all the odd religions or beliefs of the leading Republicans: on Nixon, a Quaker; Romney, a Mormon; Percy, a Christian Scientist; Hatfield, a teetotaler. In America and American politics, in this land where we worship success, these, and not Roman Catholicism, may be the true American heresies.

As for Johnson, the senator continued, while he was still majority leader, he had begun to behave less and less according to the Senate rule book and more and more according to the rules set forth in *The Territorial Imperative*, taking over increasing amounts of space in the Senate Office Building, until he had accumulated whole suites that weren't used or even inhabited, but merely staked out and branded "His."

Is *this* what U.S. senators are like? So candid? So crackling? So accessible? I did not know any other senators, but those two hours with McCarthy made me wonder what other exotic blooms might lurk in the Congressional hothouse. Most extraordinary was the rare sense of recognition that a person you have only just met is somehow already an old and close friend. The encounter had been so vivid that when we got home my mother and I played a game, each of us making notes of what had been said. Exhilarated by the rich talk in California's usually arid air, we found ourselves suffering from a joint attack of total recall.

I didn't know then that these impromptu notes would be the first of thousands I would take over the next year and a half. I didn't know then that my new friend would run for President and turn the country upside down. At lunch, that March, he had said that if Johnson didn't reverse himself by fall, but continued to widen and deepen our involvement in Vietnam, he would have to be stopped. Liberal Democrats in the Senate would not permit Johnson to continue. Many Senate doves were from the northwestern states. Watch this corner of the map, McCarthy said, and we'd see one of these men throw himself in front of the Johnson juggernaut. We didn't even suspect, then, that he himself would be the man to make the challenge, but neither, I am sure, did Senator McCarthy know it. But a year later, almost to the day, I stood by his side in Wisconsin and heard LBJ quit the race.

One of the most fascinating mysteries of 1968, in fact, was to run down the identity of the first person to get the idea of running Eugene McCarthy for President. It was like trying to track the source of the Nile. I didn't know then, in March, that I would try to solve this mystery myself. I didn't know that I would accompany the senator on his campaign—that I would be his fellow traveler, dinner partner, impromptu historian, for scores of club sandwiches and hundreds of thousands of airplane miles, crisscrossing the United States.

I didn't know that after twenty years as a reporter, through a casual friend and lunch date, I would meet my own country at last and learn something of its politics, and its people, as well as something about myself and a great deal about my old-new friend, in the simmering pressure cooker of personalities, emotions, and heightened events that is any Presidential campaign.

I put some of my first impressions and strong feelings about the senator into the first of eight pieces I was to write on him during the campaign. When this piece was published, my friend was tramping the snows of New Hampshire, invisible still to Washington and to the world, and the piece seemed as much a valedictory to a brave Quixote, already doomed, as a curtain raiser on the most interesting political adventure of our time.

New Hampshire

♥

SENATOR Eugene McCarthy is a conundrum. One's first response to him is surprise. Admiration, when it comes, comes later. The senator first surprised me when we met last March at a Washington dinner party. Subtle, wry, casual, reflective, startlingly candid, bleached of the least speck of self-importance—he seemed so various a mix of man, one wondered what he uses for mortar.

A year later I still wonder, and McCarthy continues to surprise me by letter, speech, and deed. When I wrote in this space that I liked to get letters, I got one from the senator beginning: "You are right about the need for letter-writing, especially for politicians. Our signatures deteriorate as we become less certain, or perhaps committed on too many issues, and our mechanical signatures take on authenticity."

I am always surprised by the special tilt and skew of McCarthy's mind. In a discussion of India and birth control, for example, he remarked that he would favor putting IUDs into all sacred cows.

Many surprises followed. The senator once studied to be a monk. He used to play semipro baseball. He is a theologian— and a superb poet, so good, in fact, that if McCarthy ever publishes his verse, a decision he has so far been unable to

February 1968

bring himself to make, history may remember the poet long after the politician has been forgot.

Still, none of this prepared me for McCarthy's big stunner, his decision to challenge Lyndon Johnson for the Democratic nomination for President. That one surprised every professional politician in the country including, I feel reasonably certain, the enigmatic senator himself. (He has since explained that he would find it difficult to face his children if he stood aside in 1968.)

Since his announcement McCarthy has begun to act like a presidential candidate, but he still does not look like a candidate, or at least not like the kind of vigorous, exhorting, happy gardener of grass roots we are accustomed to in American politics. George Romney out shaking hands before dawn in sub-zero weather looks like a candidate. Couturier Richard Nixon, meticulously cutting out and stitching up the Joseph's coat on civil rights that he hopes will become him equally well in North and South, looks like a candidate; a loser, but a candidate. Percy under Vietcong fire, Wallace spouting, and Bobby Kennedy playing it cool all variously look like candidates. Despite the eyes lifted in modest denial, Ronald Reagan and Nelson Rockefeller look very much like candidates too. And so does LBJ. But Eugene McCarthy, strolling campuses, reading poetry, making his low-key, rather scholarly speeches —in one here in California he likened the Watts riot to the Peasant's Revolt of 1381—looks not like a candidate but like a professor, which he also has been.

McCarthy's shortcomings as a candidate are really problems of congruity; his personal style is out of phase with our noisy and anxious times. People want to be galvanized, and they want to be told what to do. But McCarthy is not by nature galvanic: He would stimulate not by electric shock, but by the application of mind. It has also been charged that he lacks "fight," but it is thought, not fight, that is in desperately short supply today. A man like McCarthy is not only rare, he is out of fashion. He is no Eartha Kitt and no Maharishi. Simple answers don't attract him; complex questions do. Finally, there is the matter of contrast. In the Truman or even in the Woodrow Wilson era, McCarthy would not look so good. If the Goliath in the White House were less flamboyant, Mc-Carthy would not seem so attractively gray.

It is unfortunate that the senator's unfashionable look tends to obscure his sound. Even would-be supporters claim they don't really know what McCarthy stands for, although he has made that quite clear: He wants to offer his party an alterna-tive to LBJ's Vietnam policy, which McCarthy regards as immoral and destructive to the nation's character and purpose. He also hopes to demonstrate to disaffected young people that the democratic process is honest and will work. Often, glanc-ing at the morning paper, I find myself brought up short by the particular correctness of something the senator has said. In New Hampshire: "The need today is not for practical men but reflective men." In Wisconsin, when asked about polls indicating strong hawkish sentiment: "Campaigning on the issue of administration policies in Vietnam should not be determined by polls." In California: "I have not abandoned the Democratic party, but the Democratic party has abandoned the positions it took in 1964."

The senator has often been called a stalking-horse, but I think he is really a Trojan horse. He is trying to smuggle some ideas, some ideals, and some serious thought inside the tradi-tional circus tent of big-time American party politics. An election year on TV now resembles a sort of marathon Miss America contest in which the candidates—each of them confi-dent, rugged, toothpaste-smiling, ever-cheerful—parade before us their beauty, brains, poise, and ability to play a saxophone solo. McCarthy's manner is more suggestive of Emmett Kelly trying to sweep up his own spotlight. The senator's evident allergy to razzle-dazzle, the refusal to tootle his saxophone, is to me one of his more attractive aspects.

I admire the scholarly senator for a number of other things he won't do. He won't oversimplify. He won't run a rah-rah, straw-hats-and-balloons campaign, he won't orate, he won't ripsnort, and he won't demagogue.

But the complaint that one hears most often about Eugene McCarthy is that he won't win. Won't, can't, and should not divide his party by trying. I have about decided that this argument is based on a faulty understanding of what it means to "win."

What Senator McCarthy wants most is to alter the foreign policy of the United States and to repair the terrible damage to American clarity of thought that has resulted from the popularity-contest kind of campaigning. I think that simply by becoming a candidate, by stimulating people to think, to question, and to doubt, by reasserting the dominion of idea over personality and of mind over charisma, McCarthy has in his own terms begun to win already.

Wisconsin

❧

"Poets," said Shelley long ago, "are the unacknowledged legislators of the world." Today we have a legislator who is an unacknowledged poet. Unacknowledged too until now is the possibility—after Wisconsin, suddenly real—that Eugene McCarthy could be President of the United States.

There is novelty in the idea of a poet-President, but no incompatibility, for McCarthy's political strength and his verse flow from the same richness of mind. In a poem to his friend Robert Lowell, whom he brilliantly epitomizes as "poet of purity and of parsimony, using one sense at a time," the senator goes on to praise Lowell as "double agent of doubt, smuggler of truth."

That line also describes McCarthy's own style as a presidential campaigner. When he first announced his candidacy, the senator was dismissed as an unknown Don Quixote, a "gallant irrelevancy." McCarthy may have been poorly organized, and undersupplied with money, but he was never irrelevant. His candidacy came about as response, reflection, and riposte to the bleary political, moral, and social climate of the times.

In his quiet, low-voltage way McCarthy has by now put into circulation enough double-edged doubts and smuggled truths about the real state of the union to throw the political situation

April 1968

into an uproar. This mild-seeming man may or may not have scared Rocky out of the presidential race, but he certainly scared Bobby in. Now he has helped unhorse a President and perhaps toppled a policy. In four months the foolish knight has shown himself a serious prince. McCarthy is now a major political figure, and though he may not be nominated for President in 1968, or even in 1972, he will be a force to be reckoned with in America for a long time to come.

Certainly McCarthy's accelerating strength as a candidate does not come from traditional sources of political power—party patronage, great wealth, or personal charisma. It comes from the force and toughness and nobility of his ideas. McCarthy's speeches invariably are addressed to the people, not to the party. He appears less interested in the making of a President than in the making of an electorate, the putting together of what he calls a "constituency of conscience. . . . It's a new America," he says, "and we need a new kind of politics."

The Milwaukee speech on March 23, in which the Minnesota senator first presented himself as a serious candidate for President and "not just as an educational force," restated the same deep conviction that McCarthy had first articulated in his passionate nominating speech for Adlai Stevenson eight years before. He prefers leaders who are sought out by the people over leaders who seek power for themselves. "This country does not so much need leadership," he explained, "because the potential for leadership in a free country must exist in every man and every woman. The President must be prepared to be a kind of channel for [people's] aspirations . . . largely by way of setting people free."

In the same speech McCarthy for the first time made public his fondness for verse, mentioned four poets in half an hour, and concluded with the passage from Walt Whitman that has become one of his major themes: "Poets to come, and orators to come, and singers, all of you who are to come . . . arouse, arouse; for you must justify me; you must answer."

227)

McCarthy has read verse all his life, and a year or so ago he started writing it as well, scratching out lines in longhand at odd hours in planes and hotel rooms, later typing them up in his Senate office and stashing them in a scuffed blue notebook misleadingly labeled "University of Minnesota." There are fifty or more poems or fragments of poems in the folder, none published, and until recently not even shown to many other people. Humility and great respect for the company of all poets, alive and dead, account in part for his reluctance. But it is writing verse that interests him, not having it read.

Lately McCarthy has discovered, with some surprise, that people who like his politics also tend to like poetry. Crowds surge forward eagerly when they learn that Robert Lowell is traveling with the candidate. And recently, addressing a union meeting in a Milwaukee basement, the senator was astounded to hear himself proudly introduced to an audience of Amalgamated Clothing Workers and meatcutters as "The Honorable Eugene J. McCarthy—poet, friend of labor, and candidate for President of the United States!"

The tough-minded candidate and the questioning poet dwell quite compatibly in the same place—inside McCarthy's silver-gray head—along with a seasoned philosopher, a shrewd gambler, and the intense twelve-year-old whose boyhood is so vividly recollected here in a poem by the mature McCarthy:

The Day Time Began

Our days were yellow and green
we marked the seasons with respect,
but spring was ours. We were shoots
and sprouts, and greenings,
We heard the first word
that fish were running in the creek.
Secretive we went with men into sheds
for torches and tridents
for nets and traps.

Shana Alexander

We shared the wildness of that week,
in men and fish. First fruits
after the winter. Dried meat gone,
the pork barrel holding only brine.
Bank clerks came out in skins,
teachers in loin clouts,
while game wardens drove in darkened cars,
watching the vagrant flares
beside the fish mad streams, or crouched
at home to see who came and went,
holding their peace
surprised by violence.

We were spendthrift of time
A day was not too much to spend
to find a willow right for a whistle
to blow the greenest sound the world
has ever heard.
Another day to search the oak and hickory thickets,
geometry and experience run together
to choose the fork, fit
for a sling.
Whole days long we pursued the spotted frogs
and dared the curse of newts and toads.

New adams, unhurried, pure, we checked the names
given by the old.
Some things we found well titled
blood-root for sight
skunks for smell
crab apples for taste
yarrow for sound
mallow for touch.
Some we found named ill, too little or too much
or in a foreign tongue.
These we challenged with new names.

229)

Space was our preoccupation,
infinity, not eternity our concern.
We were strong bent on counting,
the railroad ties, so many to a mile,
the telephone poles, the cars that passed,
marking our growth against the door frames.

The sky was a kite,
I flew it on a string, winding
it in to see its blue, again
to count the whirling swallows,
and read the patterned scroll of blackbirds turning
to check the markings of the hawk,
and then letting it out to the end
of the last pinched inch of
string, in the vise of thumb and finger.

One day the string broke,
the kite fled over the shoulder of the world,
but reluctantly, reaching back in great lunges
as lost kites do, or as a girl running
in a reversed movie, as at each arched step, the earth
set free, leaps forward, catching
her farther back
the treadmill doubly betraying,
Remote and more remote.

Now I lie on a west facing hill in October
the dragging string having circled the world, the universe,
crosses my hand in the grass. I do not grasp it,
it brushes my closed eyes, I do not open
That world is no longer mine, but for remembrance
Space ended then, and time began.

The mind that contains all these elements is a complex place:
hall of mirrors, citadel of faith, archive of facts, sardonic fun-

house, pragmatist's pad, thinker's tower, and something of a hermit's cell.

Yet for all the depth and passion of mind that his verse suggests, McCarthy has the true dignity of a still surface, a composure that, in the hurly-burly of politics, is a really difficult thing to achieve. The easy thing is to demagogue. But McCarthy has the true poet's style of mind—oblique, comfortable in ambiguity, informed by paradox. This, and not policy or program, is perhaps the greatest difference between him and Robert Kennedy. It is a matter of fundamental style. Kennedy shoots; McCarthy fishes. McCarthy doesn't want to sock it to 'em. "I don't want them to scream, I want them to listen. Bobby's campaign is like a grass fire—it will just burn off the surface. Mine is like a fire in a peat bog. It will hold on for six months."

A half year before he decided to offer himself as a candidate for President, in the time when he was still hoping fervently that someone else would step forward to protest the policies and patterns that McCarthy opposed, the senator wrote the following poem:

Lament of an Aging Politician

The Dream of Gerontion is my dream
And Lowell's self-salted
night sweat, wet, flannel, my morning's
shoulder shroud.

Now, far-sighted I see the distant danger
beyond the coffin confines of telephone booths,
my arms stretched to read, in vain.

Stubbornness and penicillin hold
the aged above me.
My metaphors grow cold and old,
my enemies, both young and bold.

231)

I have left Act I, for involution
and Act II. There mired in complexity
I cannot write Act III.

A day or two before the Wisconsin primary, the senator was driving through a long, bare stretch of Wisconsin farmland. The plowed fields were black earth and straw, the bare trees were black etchings on sky, and he noticed crows, a black dog, black cows. "Black is the true color of early spring," he said. "It's the only color you really see."

I asked if he still felt unable to write Act III. "I don't really want to write it," he said. "You know the old rules: Act I states the problem, Act II deals with the complications, and Act III resolves them. I'm an Act II man. That's where I live— involution and complexity.

"In politics, I think you must stay in Act II. You can't draw lines under things, or add up scores; the complications just go on in different forms. You have to understand that. When you get into Act III, you have to write a tragedy. Napoleon tried writing Act III, and in the last year of his life I think Woodrow Wilson attempted it. He wanted to wrap the world all up, just when he was coming apart.

"FDR never quite came to that point, drawing a line under the score and adding things up, because he always moved on to new problems."

The senator paused to point out a few bare tamaracks by the roadside. These can grow only in marginal land, between swamp and field, and they cannot seed themselves within their own shadow. McCarthy thinks them the saddest of trees, and another of his poems speaks of "the least trees in that least land."

"No, I'd say Roosevelt was an Act II politician," he went on, happy at being able, upon reflection, to include Franklin Roosevelt in his favorite category.

I asked him about other Presidents. "Lyndon only really

cares about Act III. What does history say about the Great Society? What will the future think of Lyndon Johnson?

"With Eisenhower you just got the sound of the orchestra tuning up all the time. Jack Kennedy brought a style to the Presidency, a proper sense of the office, but he really didn't get time to write much.

"Bobby is an Act I man. He says here's a problem. Here's another problem. Here's another. He never really deals with Act II, but I think maybe Bobby's beginning to write Act III now. Bobby's tragedy is that to beat me, he's going to have to destroy his brother. Today I occupy most of Jack's positions on the board. That's kind of Greek, isn't it?"

He looked out the window now, pointing out features of the glacial moraine, the clay hills, the hollowed-out swamps where the tamarack grows, and the thickets of pussy willow signaling with their faint claret haze the very first color of Midwest spring. "Well, here we go again, making rash judgments all across Wisconsin," he said with a grin.

Indiana

❧

Eugene McCarthy is a politician with a poet's eye, which, like
an eye of Argus, never closes. Though the politician works
with others, the poet works alone, jotting brief images in a
spiral notebook.

Long underwear suits freeze on a New Hampshire clothes-
line like dry bones. The sugar maples yield midwinter hope.
Though they look more dead than any other tree, the sap is
rising; they are really most alive.

I do not, of course, suggest that McCarthy, the practiced
politician, proceeds toward the White House by entrail-
gazing, only that in the terrible rigors of a presidential campaign, the senator has worked out a congenial arrangement
between the public and the private man. Verse refreshes the
groggy campaigner, and politics weights the poet's pen.

His poet's eye served McCarthy particularly well in Indiana,
an inscrutable and frustrating place for all of the out-of-state
candidates. Hoosiers are closemouthed, provincial, and suspi-
cious of outsiders. Their governor refers to presidential candidates as "foreign invaders." From the air, Indiana looks plump
and green, and Indianapolis pokes up in the center, smug as
Jack Horner's thumb. But at ground level, the city becomes a
dense thicket of oversize advertising signs. Some whizbang
salesman must have passed through town, and now each block
bristles with lofty movie marquees that proclaim things like

May 1968

SAUSAGE 2 EGG 50¢. "This is kind of a crazy state, you know," McCarthy remarked one day. "The people don't like to tell you what they think, and it's a place with no form, no borders. To reach Indianans on TV, you have to buy time in Chicago or Louisville."

During the frustrating and baffling weeks before the Indiana primary, the poet's eye came to see the state as a place of good signs and bad signs. "The people here don't cut down the lilac bushes, as they have in other states, and they leave big trees standing in the plowed fields. They like music, too. Those are good signs." Later he sketched out some verses on signs he liked least.

Three Bad Signs

The first Bad Sign is this:
"Green River Ordinance Enforced Here.
Peddlers Not Allowed."

This is a clean, safe town.
No one can just come round.
With ribbons and bright thread
Or new books to be read
This is an established place.
We have accepted patterns in lace,
And ban itinerant vendors of new forms and whirls,
All things that turn the heads of girls.
We are not narrow, but we live with care.
Gypsies, hawkers and minstrels are right for a fair.
But transient peddlers, nuisances, we say
From Green River must be kept away.
Traveling preachers, actors with a play,
Can pass through, but may not stay.
Phoenicians, Jews, men of Venice—
Know that this is the home of Kiwanis.
All you who have been round the world to find

Beauty in small things: read our sign
And move on.

The second Bad Sign is this:
"Mixed Drinks."

"Mixed Drinks."
What mystery blinks
As in the thin blood of the neon sign
The uncertain hearts of the customers
Are tested there in the window.
Embolism after embolism, repeating,
Mixed drinks between the art movie
And the Reasonable Rates Hotel.
Mixed drinks are class,
Each requires a different glass.
Mixed drink is manhattan red
Between the adult movie and the unmade bed
Mixed drink is daiquiri green
Between the gospel mission and the sheen
Of hair oil on the rose planted paper.
Mixed drink is remembrance between
                              unshaded
40-watt bulbs hung from the ceiling,
Between the light a man cannot live by.
And the better darkness.
Mixed drink is the sign of contradiction.

The third Bad Sign is this:
"We Serve All Faiths."

We serve all faiths:
We the morticians.
Tobias is out, he has had it.
We do not bury the dead.
Not, He died, was buried and after three
                    days arose.

(236

But he died, was revived, and after three
  days was buried alive.
This is our scripture.
Do not disturb the established practitioner.
Do not disturb the traditional mortician:
Giving fans to the church, for hot days,
Dropping a calendar at the nursing home,
A pamphlet in the hospital waiting room,
An ad in the testimonial brochure at the retirement banquet.
Promising the right music, the artificial grass.
We bury faith of all kinds.
Foreverness does not come easily.
The rates should be higher.

The Indiana primary produced no really good signs or bad signs for any of the candidates. After it was over, McCarthy flew to Nebraska, a region he likes, among other reasons, because it is open and "because, if you listen, you can hear cattle moving anyplace in the state. Or it may be buffalo."

Nebraska will mark the fourth time McCarthy offers himself to the people in what he has calculated are nine steps to the Presidency—seven state primary contests, the Democratic convention, and the general election in November.

"Look up the ancient Chinese poem about cranes," he told a friend before he left. "The crane was sacred to poetry and to peace. It takes nine steps before it flies.

"Some birds take no steps before they fly. A pigeon just jumps up. Like Bobby."

Nebraska

🌱

"POPE had it all wrong, you know. The proper study of mankind is animals."

It was Primary Day in Nebraska, and Eugene McCarthy was relaxing by doing two of the things he enjoys most: walking down a country railroad track, and skylarking with words. To accompany the senator on such a ramble is a little like strolling through cornfields with Aesop or La Fontaine, for McCarthy's talk is a continuing stream of animal metaphor. In it beasts lope or slither or plod by, tails flick, wings flap, hooves pound, creatures crawl and creep, each animal coming along just on cue to animate the precise image McCarthy seeks.

A man of subtle and elastic mind, McCarthy uses many kinds of metaphor. Animals, trees, rocks, baseball, and the lives of the saints serve him well. But his fun in talking politics comes from talking it in animal terms, and on that brief Nebraska afternoon, cows, pigs, blackbirds, a skunk, and a rooster all turned up in Senator McCarthy's cornfield parade.

"You know the difference between how you move cows and how you move pigs, don't you?" he begins. "You drive cows by starting slow and quiet, and then you increase the tempo until you have a stampede. To move pigs, you have to holler and beat on the trough to get their attention, but then you

May 1968

must slow down until you almost walk them in." Then, without warning: "I think people are more like pigs than they are like cattle."

"Another thing about a pig," he goes on, "he thinks he's warm if his nose is warm. I saw a bunch of pigs one time that had frozen to death in a rosette, each one's nose tucked under the rump of the one in front." Pause. "We have a lot of pigs in politics."

The reporters who follow McCarthy's campaign trail are blackbirds sitting on a telephone wire: When one flies away they all fly away; when one sits down again they all come back.

Lyndon Johnson uses other people's organizations, like the cowbird that lays its eggs in other birds' nests. "The secret is that the cowbird's eggs hatch first. So by the time the others hatch, the bird's too big to throw out. The question is: How many nests can you use up before the other birds get wise?"

The trouble with the administration's poverty program is that it moves forward like a rooster. When it lifts its leg it seems to be taking an enormous stride, "but when he puts the foot down, it's right by the other one."

The proper way to catch a skunk is to poke a strand of barbed wire down its hole, twist it until you engage the skunk's tail, and pull. "A skunk shaking its tail is dangerous, but a tail shaking a skunk is no threat at all." Ah, metaphors all.

If McCarthy's teeming verbal ark does not capsize and sink somewhere along the voyage to the White House, he will surely be our most animal-haunted President since Abraham Lincoln, as well as our sharpest-tongued President. In the Lincoln-Douglas debates, Douglas was never a senator but always a toothless lion, a frightened bear, a cuttlefish. Lincoln did not say, "I will pardon the prisoners," but, "I will turn out the flock." After Gettysburg he did not say, "General, you let the enemy escape across the Potomac," but, "Meade, it seems to me you shooed the geese over the river." Slavery to Lincoln

239)

was sometimes an ant, sometimes a whale which "with one flop of his tail . . . will send us all into eternity."

Generally speaking, McCarthy's animals tend to be humbler and less apocalyptic creatures than Lincoln's. He usually sticks to farm animals and the creatures of the woods and fields he knew in his Minnesota boyhood. "I may be the last country boy left," he often laments now, and he wonders wryly what will happen to metaphor in a world where people say, as one of his young campaign workers recently did, that a lovely mountain lake reminded her of a Hamm's beer ad.

McCarthy also shares the farmer's long-range and slow-cycled view of events, and so the morning after the primary results came in, the senator seemed not in the least depressed by the sizable Nebraska vote his two Democratic rivals received. Hubert Humphrey, he thought, was like a dog that barks and sits up without being asked. "He wants the office so bad, you want to give it to him." It was more difficult for McCarthy to find an animal image for Bobby. He settled reluctantly on the wolverine, even though "Bobby is only in some ways like a wolverine."

What ways, I asked, and the senator said, "Well, it's a kind of a torn animal. It doesn't really know its identity. It fouls up traps, or destroys what's in a trap, and its frightening snarl scares trappers in lonely camps."

McCarthy's parade of animals marches on into his verse, and it is not irrelevant that the most serious of his poems, "Communions," is a haunting complication of beast, man, and God.

Communions

> Gentle the deer with solicitude
> Solace them with salt
> Comfort them with apples
> Prepare them for the rectitude
> Of Man who will come
> A stranger with the unfamiliar gun.

(240

Shana Alexander

The watcher calls. In trust the head
                                    turns.
Between the antlers St. Hubert's cross
                                    burns.
No Conversion today—but quick shot.
The buck falls to his knees
In decent genuflection to death.
                    The doe flees.
He is not dead. He will arise.
In three weeks, the head
Will look through the wall
But with changed eyes.

But what of the body of swiftness
And litheness. Oh. Witness
Ground heart and muscle
Intestinal cased, tied with gristle,
The sausage sacrament of Communion.
So that all may share the guilt of one
Under the transplanted eyes
                    of the watcher.

The poem is about deer hunting in Texas. But whether or not
it was inspired by a Christmas recipe for deer sausage beginning "one half deer, one half hog" that was sent out to friends
from the LBJ Ranch, the author does not say. Everyone has a
right to poetical, if not political, obscurity.

Oregon

✤

"WELL, we got Big Shorty," Mary McCarthy, the senator's cool-eyed daughter, told her father in Wisconsin on the night that Lyndon Johnson quit the race. "Now we gotta get Little Shorty."

In Oregon, they got him. Eugene McCarthy's victory over Robert Kennedy was the first time any Kennedy had been defeated in any primary, ever, and if Bobby was not quite firmly knocked out yet, he was "pretty well bloodied up."

That phrase was Clean Gene's own, and anybody who is surprised at its pugnacity doesn't know the McCarthys. Like his daughter, the senator has always concealed a hearty taste for combat behind that impeccable cool. Throughout the Oregon campaign, a new fighting spirit infused the entire McCarthy camp. "I'm more of a caveman than you are," poet Robert Lowell told a Cro-Magnon-suited booster at one stop. But McCarthy was in some ways more of a caveman than anybody, and he was enjoying it. Of his front-seat canoe ride he said, "I would have been the first one shot from ambush, if there had been an ambush." Instead, there was one of the greatest upsets in presidential politics since the night Harry Truman defeated the Little Shorty of 1948. And when Kennedy's defeat was confirmed, and a reporter asked whether McCarthy would now consider Hubert Humphrey his principal opponent, McCarthy said icily, "He always was my principal opponent."

Much later on that very important night in the drama of both men's lives, a night which seemed to free each one from his own old ghost at last, long after the most tireless reporters had gone to bed and the last jubilant supporter had stopped shouting underneath the windows of his hotel suite, McCarthy talked more about his and Kennedy's battle tactics.

"There always comes a time when you ought to change your weapons," he said. "Yet people hang on to the weapons of the old heroes until they lose a war. The British kept the longbow and the Persians kept the short spear. The Romans kept the phalanx until Hannibal brought in elephants. Bobby tried to beat me with a dog and an astronaut."

In his Oregon speeches, McCarthy had hammered repeatedly at the important distinction between mistakes and misconceptions. "Senator Kennedy has said he has made mistakes. Much more serious than a mistake is a misconception. You can say, 'I'm sorry about that particular wiretap.' But what about the *idea* of wiretap?"

Bobby's mistake about his own campaign, McCarthy thinks, was always the failure to distinguish himself from the larger Kennedy image. "Bobby should have stayed up on the high ground. He might have been better off to make the case for himself, all the way. What happened in Oregon was that these voters were the first ones to see him clearly as the senator from New York, rather than as some sort of general configuration involving his brother. He used things like the dog and the space man and his mother to try to condition people to see that configuration."

Bobby's misconception was to assume that his outworn style of politicking would still work. McCarthy believes that the final victory for such old-style politics, ironically, was Jack Kennedy's own win in 1960. After that, the weapons changed.

McCarthy is convinced that the proper way and indeed the only way to reach today's voters is to speak to them directly,

243)

to deal plainly with the issues, and to make a total and open personal commitment. New politics means to him that the candidate must be entirely open himself. Since these are, of course, the same old weapons he has been using since New Hampshire, he feels he might have pulled ahead sooner if he hadn't had to make two starts, the second one after President Johnson pulled out of the race. The night that happened, the stunned senator remarked, "I feel as if I've been tracking a tiger through long jungle grass, and all of a sudden he rolls over and he's stuffed." It took him until Oregon to find his stride again, and now that he is off and running, he very much hopes that both Humphrey and Kennedy will stay in. "It's so disconcerting when the other horse jumps the fence and starts to graze."

McCarthy's ultimate weapon in this campaign, more potent even than the force of his ideas, the patent sincerity of his commitment, his courage, or even the pull of his strange, cool personality, may be his utter detachment about the prize he seeks. The office of the Presidency interests him: The job does not. Back in Indiana he had said, "Nothing is more dangerous than a man with no ambition. Especially if he happens to be running for President under rather, ah, peculiar circumstances." A further paradox in a dizzying campaign already bristling with more ironies than a shelf of Greek plays is that the one man who might find it most difficult to believe that Eugene McCarthy really doesn't want the job in the White House is Robert F. Kennedy.

Abigail McCarthy, the senator's wife, shares his paradoxical, turned-around views and ways of stating things. "Gene is an antihero," she told me that last night in Oregon. "I think he has to be. This country can't afford any more heroes."

But it may have been Mary McCarthy who had the last and coolest word: "If I had known things were going to get this serious, I never would have gone in."

New York

❧

NINE nights after the assassination, seeming more alone now than ever, more alone even than when he trudged the snows of New Hampshire, Eugene McCarthy resumed his campaign for the Presidency of the United States. In New York a week before the primary that McCarthy was to win so big, a sellout crowd jammed the hotel corridors and ballroom to watch the senator's reentry into the lists. So many security men were present, a flight of tropical butterflies appeared to have alighted on the throng. Lapels by the hundreds bloomed with the red, white, and blue triangles of the Secret Service, the red and yellow insignia of the Treasury agents, the cerulean and white stickpins of the city detectives, some cream and turquoise buttons, perhaps from U.N.C.L.E., and the new orange-and blue striped shamrocks of the wan-faced McCarthy staff. "He wanted to tear down the fences around the White House—and now look!" one tearful McCarthy girl cried, waving an arm toward the riotous profusion of fuzz.

The candidate himself looked grayer than ever. His voice suggested deep emotion netted in tightest control. The crowd seemed to share his mood, the big room so quiet that whenever the senator paused to raise his eyes from his text, the sharp burst of camera clicks printed a dotted line across the silence. His words had an elegiac tone, as when he spoke of the need to

June 1968

"take our steel out of the land of thatched huts, and our tanks out of the land of water buffalo and bicycles, and our napalm out of the land that scarcely knows the use of matches."

The next day passengers aboard the campaign plane for a three-day tour of western states could feel a deep melancholy diffusing from the candidate himself. It seemed more than simple grief. It was as if he had just no stomach left, and no heart, for whatever it is a man must do to win votes in this land. Despite his nine-day respite from campaigning, McCarthy seemed more weary now than he had on the somber California morning he bid good-bye to his staff in the heavily guarded corridor of his hotel, parting from each good friend with a brief, firm embrace, as if *he* were reassuring *them*.

Now the candidate himself needed reassurance, and neither his friends nor his devoted young staff nor the warm crowds that had gathered at each stop seemed able to provide it. Perhaps only a tough and worthy opponent could do that. "I feel like the Black Knight out in the center of the field," he said one time. "I turn my horse round and round, but there is no one to fight. I go to their tents to strike their shields with my lance, but not even a shield hangs there now. Only flapping rags."

Other metaphors said it differently. He felt he was competing in a nightmare Grand Prix where the drivers change each time around, but the race never ends. He said he felt that he had the ball and had to keep running forever, running past the fifty-yard line and on and on because there was no goal line. He said he felt like the losing dice player in the sixth canto of Dante's *Purgatorio*, who keeps on shooting after everyone else has gone home.

Hoping to cheer him up, someone mentioned that soon Hubert Humphrey would be back on the field. "He's the kind of opponent I really like," McCarthy said ruefully. "I think I know his weaknesses better than he knows mine. But now I'm going to have to use sixteen-ounce gloves and one of those Archie Moore belts that come up to about the fifth rib."

The candidate's sense of aimlessness and drift was shared by everyone aboard the plane. The only passengers who seemed certain of what they were doing there were the Secret Service men. McCarthy said it felt like sitting around the gym after the big game, when nobody wants to take off his sweat shirt. Some observers felt the truth was that McCarthy was really tormented by deep guilts about Robert Kennedy. I disagree. I think McCarthy knows that some men by their nature are driven to put on the kind of charisma suit that serves as a lightning rod to violence. I think what gripped McCarthy was not a sense of guilt, but an overwhelming sense of Greek tragedy playing itself out.

As the plane moved on from Idaho and Montana through Arizona and New Mexico, it became evident that part of the letdown we all felt was due to the inevitable changeover from the tempo and tactics of primary-fighting to the quieter sport of delegate-hunting. In each state now, McCarthy asks his audiences to give some thought to what it really means to represent people, whether you represent them as President, or in the Senate, or as a delegate to your party's convention. Pleading for a genuinely "open" convention, he asks them not to worry about splitting their party, because "dividing Democrats in 1968 is like chopping sawdust," and to keep in mind their obligations to people as well as to party. He spoke to the delegates as people, not as units in the game of party politics, and that itself seemed to return some focus to the senator's campaign.

But most refreshing was an impromptu, unscheduled return to McCarthy's home state. He drove nearly two hours through quiet Minnesota farmlands to inspect tornado damage in the little town of Tracy. On that long Sunday drive McCarthy spoke with growing animation about the new foals he saw romping and resting in the pastures, about the wild roses you will always find growing along the railroad right-of-way, and about all the yellow mustard and green thistle that his father had made him, as a boy, chop out of the cornfields.

The sky was flat, with thick clouds floating upside down in an enormous blue bowl that touched the horizon all around. The first time he went to live in Washington, in 1944, Mc-Carthy said, he rode a bus way out of town just to see the horizon again.

He mentioned politics only once, to say that since last November when he decided to run for President, things seemed to have come full circle. Despite the thud on thud of cataclysmic events outside his campaign, the real issues hadn't changed. The war was still on. Nothing had really been done about the poverty program.

"What has changed, the past few months, is the mood of the country. It's different now. There is hope that in some way people *can* be set free."

Washington, D.C.

✤

A SCANT week before the Democratic convention, it begins to look as if Eugene McCarthy, "the man the people found," may in Chicago become the man the party dumped.

If true, this tells us more about the decrepitude of our political system than it does about the viability of a candidate who has come through the longest and possibly the wildest campaign in American Presidential history scarcely even breathing hard. In seven mad months the unknown senator from Minnesota has established himself through polls and primaries as the most popular Presidential candidate of either party. Between New Hampshire winter and convention summer, frost changed to fire, and now to millions of people a man who was invisible in snow seems inevitable in August. Yet party professionals still find McCarthy invisible; most pros confidently predict the nomination of Hubert Humphrey on the first ballot. If this is the case, next week's spectacle in the stockyards will be even more painful to watch than the arrogant tedium of Miami.

Not that the Democrats have a corner on political decrepitude. Rockefeller and Lindsay also are politicians admired by the voters and scorned by the pros of their party. But though he gathered himself up once or twice, Lindsay never leaped. Rockefeller appeared to leap without gathering himself. His

August 1968

New Politics were more non-politics: a gallant man marching on Miami waving a handful of polls and crying, "Take me!"

McCarthy on the other hand has run a full campaign and submitted himself and his policies to the test of the primaries in seven states. His popularity with the people continues to rise, and the recent McCarthy rallies I have watched from Sacramento to Saint Louis, all thickly abloom with exuberant homemade signs, seem to me the only truly spontaneous political demonstrations I have seen in years.

The absurd snake dancing after Nixon's nomination had all the spontaneity of peristalsis, and the only Republican convention speaker who seemed to me fully human was a young man who ended his address by thanking the stupefied delegates for their inattention. The final annunciation of Agnew suggested that these delegates had been inattentive not only to one another, but to the entire democratic process.

For his own "spontaneous demonstration" in Chicago next week, Senator McCarthy thinks he may send a single man out onto the floor carrying a sign, "New Hampshire: He Walked Alone"; then another solitary sign-bearer proclaiming, "Wisconsin: Tested in the Cold"; then perhaps two or three young mothers saying "He Brought Our Children Home," or some of his attractive young people walking with flowers and blowing flutes. Behind the senator's gentle mockery lurks the scary implication that the process by which we pick our leaders has become as absurd as the antics.

This process ultimately depends on that most dimly defined figure in American politics—the national delegate. Party hacks and political idealists, rubber stamps and fat-cat givers, they come in every shape and size, and they are chosen in all sorts of ways. More than three thousand of them are now converging on Chicago, baggage bulging with funny hats and redeemable promises. Most nonpolitical Americans know almost nothing about how our party system works. They don't know, for example, that a delegate pays all his own convention and travel expenses and is assessed for "hospitality" expenses as well.

More importantly, it is not clear who the delegate's constituents are. Does his primary loyalty belong to the voters he theoretically represents or to the party bosses whom he has traditionally served?

Senator McCarthy turned his attention to delegates. Invariably he talks to them as human beings, not as programmed, or programmable, atoms of the party machine. Their dim response suggests that they may not appreciate this unorthodox approach.

I found it immensely likable, and effective, when I heard McCarthy tell a group of Montana delegates last June that for the first time in his twenty years in politics, and in the fifteen years he could remember before that, "We Democrats have been taking positions which did not have the people behind us." In sum, he said that the party of the people was betraying the people, and he quietly urged his listeners "to give some thought to what it means to represent people—whether you are a president, or a senator, or a delegate."

Since Montana's delegation heads to Chicago with only two committed and three "leaning" to McCarthy out of a total of twenty-six, I suppose we will see the whale swallow Jonah after all. But if it does, it merely transports him to higher ground.

Sometimes I wonder if 1968 may not be the delegates' last stand. They remind me a bit of the last buffalo: shaggy, old, worn-out, and almost overrun, the old boss bulls standing in a circle with great moth-eaten faces facing outward to protect the rest of the herd. I feel sorry for them then, and I tell myself that if it is true that the people are to be locked out of the convention hall—as much by the archaic structure of party politicians as by Mayor Daley's cops—it is equally true that the delegates are locked in.

Perhaps it is not too late. Perhaps the process can still be made to work. McCarthy thinks we need to open up the system, to have proportional representation all the way up to the top, rather than to cut it off at the precinct level as both parties now do. Instead of perpetuating a system based on past loyalties, we ought to find a way to let new forces and new blood come in: young people, suburbanites, the disenfranchised poor. He suggests the parties hold conventions every two years instead of every four, and points out that the candidates would have more time to deal with issues if the parties assumed certain fund-raising and public relations functions of politics.

The three-thousand-odd buffalo now converging on Chicago may be too old to change, but I continue to believe in a last chance and to hope that even these party pros will respond as citizens first, and delegates second. If they hold a truly open convention, they can invalidate the cynical prophecy heard for months around McCarthy headquarters that there now exists a man in America who can surely be elected in November, but cannot possibly be nominated in August.

Chicago

🌸

CHICAGO last week was a vast lockup—pigs locked in the stockyards and delegates locked in the convention hall, antiwar demonstrators locked in the park, guests locked in the Kafka Hilton across the way, politicians locked into the Party, and everybody locked into the System. Barbed wire and party loyalties built barricades. Blue policemen and shuttered minds made ugly, unbreachable walls. When at last Hubert Humphrey and Edmund Muskie had been ceremonially gaveled by their party into the positions they will occupy at least until November, some politicians who had previously seemed locked out now seemed locked in. But the old walls still stood, and the only man who looked as free after the convention ended as he had looked before it began was the man who lost, Eugene McCarthy.

By Wednesday morning, everybody knew McCarthy could not win. But having observed the extremely modest birth of his campaign last November and admired the exuberant growth which followed, my own sense of symmetry as well as my ongoing regard for the man required me to be there at the close.

In the McCarthy family suite, the senator and his brother were tossing an orange around, but they weren't just playing catch. The candidate was covering first base with the orange,

September 1968

making some fairly fancy leaps and stabs and dives at the hurtling fruit. McCarthy was a professional first baseman long before he became a professional politician, and what interests him most is style. In stylistic potential, he says, no other position can touch first base. It is the difference between a bunch of high jumpers and Nijinsky. Off and on through that long last day, as the tensions in the city grew, the McCarthy clan stayed loose and the oranges flew.

On the first-base side of their big twenty-third-floor suite, a big window overlooked Grant Park, where the demonstrators were gathering. Behind home plate glowed the color television set, an electronic picture window into the convention hall. "It's like the last stand of the old buffaloes out there," McCarthy said. "They're rump against rump now, so they can't back up, and if one pulls out, they all fall over."

Then he pointed down to the park. "The worst thing about what's happening is that it leaves those kids no place to go."

Interruptions and citrus frailty made it a long, six-orange day, the game a ticking orange time bomb linking the politicians in the hall to the people in the park. Each time we checked the window, more demonstrators and blue police filled the green scene. At dusk the last view from the window looked like a medieval army of knights and foot soldiers, with a painted blue lake in the background. Then the painted people began to move, the gas rose, the colors blurred.

For the rest of the night television told one story, truth another. On TV, a nice bunch of McCarthy rooters held up a bright blue daisy chain of McCarthy stickers. Through floodlit feathery treetops we watched other kids flee the blue police. Faint screams from the street were drowned out by fake hoopla on the screen. Nominating McCarthy, Iowa's Governor Hughes said, "He used no man's muscle but his own." In the park, nightsticks swung. In his noble seconding speech, Julian Bond said, "Not only could he hear the truth, he knew we were starving for it." Below, sharp bayonet shadows sliced the floodlit glare.

(254

Shana Alexander

"Could you believe it would end like this, Gene?" someone asked.

"No," he said, and left the room.

I went down now to the emergency first-aid rooms on the fifteenth floor and watched badly beaten kids being treated in front of TV sets still braying the happy word from the stockyards. Hotel towels had been torn up for pressure dressings, ice buckets were splash basins, and windows here were flung wide, so the gassed kids could breathe. On Michigan Boulevard we heard a phalanx of street sweepers roll by, erasing the blood on the hotel doorstep before the delegates returned.

The most appalling sight of the night was a pale and shaking young medic in blood-splashed white from head to foot, who was led in with a bleeding scalp and a broken arm and lay fainting on a hotel bed. Word of the terror must at last have penetrated the convention hall, for beyond the wounded medic's toes the TV face of Chicago's mayor loomed. "We never respond with violence," he rasped, and the ghostly, blood-spattered apparition on the bed sprang bolt upright, shrieking, "Bullshit, Daley!"

Senator McCarthy now paid a brief visit to the first-aid station, and what he saw there enraged him. "It didn't have to be this way," he said. "It's not the fault of the police so much as it is the arrogance of the convention, in refusing to let these people have any voice. It's what we've warned them about all along." In his anger he was ready to quit the party.

The senator called Blair Clark and Dick Goodwin, his managers on the convention floor. "You just can't have this kind of division in the country," he told them, and asked if they agreed he should withdraw his name from nomination, in hope that it would reduce tensions and have a stabilizing effect. "Think it over ten minutes and call me back," he said.

But, as always, McCarthy made up his own mind. "Hell, I think we ought to get out of this thing," he snapped, and put in an urgent call to Governor Harold Hughes. By now,

255)

though, the roll call had begun, and in the very early states McCarthy was doing well.

"Harold, I think if we're still ahead when we get to Iowa, you should take me out. If not, just let it run."

Certain now that he wanted to quit, he felt he could not if he were already too far behind, lest it appear he was running away. By Georgia, he knew he was losing quite badly, so he elected to stay in.

This final quixotic gesture of McCarthy's long and brave campaign was in character. Speaking quietly and calmly, one foot up on the telephone table, shoulders relaxed and a bit stooped, he looked very much like the old ballplayer he is. Certainly his last gesture had style, and thinking about it, I remembered a dispute between a couple of young McCarthy volunteers I'd overheard last spring.

"He is our last hope," one boy said.

"No, he is our first hope," said the other.

On this closing night of the longest, most grueling, and politically effective campaign in American Presidential history, I knew the second boy was right.

Epilogue

❧

Lament of an Aging Politician

The Dream of Gerontion is my dream
And Lowell's self-salted
night sweat, wet, flannel, my morning's
shoulder shroud.

Now, far-sighted I see the distant danger
beyond the coffin confines of telephone booths,
my arms stretched to read, in vain.

Stubbornness and penicillin hold
the aged above me.
My metaphors grow cold and old,
my enemies, both young and bold.

I have left Act I, for involution
and Act II. There mired in complexity
I cannot write Act III.

Eugene McCarthy

Act III is the one that resolves the problem. But this play is not over yet. That, I think, is the point of this conception of the drama. Despite the bloody violence of Chicago, and the self-destruction of the Democratic party, Chicago was not

257)

really tragedy. It had too much stupidity in it for that, too much was farcical and dumb and drained of meaning—including the party's own candidate, who set off then on his awful campaign of smiles, Happy Hubert with his politics of joy, a pathetic, grinning sort of Johnny Appleseed, spreading his need-to-please over the land.

No, the play is not over. The Nixon era is an interlude, not an act. Nixon is playing his shadow drama in Act I before the drawn curtain, while we wait for four years to discover what the real players are going to do when they reappear. Who will the real players be, when the real Act III begins, and ends? What will become of McCarthy? Is there any blood left in him? *Was* there any ever, in fact, or was he mostly the gray embodiment of all our best hopes, better instincts, for what our country should be like, for what a politician should be? Did he perhaps even know this and, his own taste for blood being gone then anyway, offer himself up for human sacrifice, hoping—if he hoped anything for himself—respite from boredom, refuge from staleness? No, Act III is still to be played, and if McCarthy knows what will happen, he isn't saying. "I'm an Act II man, myself," he had said. "That's where I live." By living there, still, he proves it. Just now the Invisible Man is hiding again: Yet has he ever been so conspicuous?